Contents

How to use this book

Start by writing your name on the front cover – this workbook has been designed for you!

You can use it as you progress through your GCSE Religious Studies course, or as part of your revision for the final exam. It's full of different activities to help you learn by doing, not just reading.

This workbook covers Paper 2, which is Component 2A: Thematic studies through the perspective of Christianity and Islam.

This refers to pages in these student books. You can go back to your student books to read about the topic in more depth.

Activity
 Christianity: pages 2–3
Islam: pages 2–3

Working your way through these activities will help strengthen your understanding of some of the key topics in your GCSE course.

Follow the instructions and write your answers in the space provided.

_____

_____

_____

Challenge activity
 Christianity: pages 2–3
Islam: pages 2–3

If you really want to stretch yourself, have a go at these challenge activities.

Follow the instructions and write your answers in the space provided.

_____

_____

There are lots of blank lines for you to write in your answers.

Key terms
 Christianity: pages 2–3
Islam: pages 2–3

It's important to get to grips with some of the specialist language that we use when talking about religion. You will need to recognise these 'key terms' because they may turn up in an exam question. And you will also need to know how to use them in your answers. These activities will help you to feel confident using religious language. Test yourself regularly on these terms.

Key Terms Glossaries appear at the end of chapters 1-6.

Key Terms Glossary
You can collect the meanings of key terms here so you can refer to them at any time. You will also be creating a useful revision tool.

Sources of religious belief and teaching

 Christianity: pages 2–3
Islam: pages 2–3

The 5-mark question in the exam asks you to 'refer to scripture or another source of Christian/Muslim belief and teaching.' These activities will help you to memorise short quotations from religious sources, such as the Bible or the Qur'an, and also explain what these quotations mean.

This will also be helpful for the 4-mark and 12-mark questions because you can refer to religious teachings to add detail to the points you make, and to back up your arguments.

TIP

Keep an eye out for these TIPS. They contain useful advice, especially to help with your exam.

Exam practice

If you see an arrow running down the side of a box, that means the activity or activities you are doing will end with an exam practice question. These are like the questions that you will encounter in your exams. Use the information and guidance from the activities to practise the 1, 2, 4, 5 and 12-mark questions.

Finally, there is a whole chapter dedicated to

Exam practice

There are five different types of question in the AQA exam paper – the **1**, **2**, **4**, **5** and **12-mark** questions.

Work your way through this chapter to find out what each question will look like and how it is marked.

There are some activities that will help you to understand what the examiner is looking for in an answer, and activities that practise the skills you should be demonstrating. You should then be ready to have a go at a few questions yourself.

WHAT WILL THE QUESTION LOOK LIKE?

This explains the command words that the question will use.

HOW IS IT MARKED?

This explains what the examiner will be looking for in your answer.

(!) REMEMBER...

This provides useful tips to help raise your marks.

All answers can be found online at **www.oxfordsecondary.co.uk/aqa-rs-answers**, so you can mark what you've done.

Once you have filled out this workbook, you will have made your own book to revise from. That's why your name is on the cover.

Chapter 1: **Theme A: Relationships and families**

Activity 1.1: Homosexuality in the UK

Christianity: pages 68–69
Islam: pages 56–57

1885	Sexual acts between homosexuals are made illegal
1967	Homosexual acts are declared legal for people over 21, except in the armed forces
1994	Age of consent for homosexual acts is reduced to 18
2000	Homosexuals are allowed to serve in the armed forces
2001	Age of consent for homosexual acts is reduced to 16
2004	Civil partnerships are recognised in law for same-sex couples
2013	Same-sex marriage is recognised in law in England and Wales
2014	Same-sex marriage is recognised in law in Scotland
2015	Same-sex marriage is recognised in law in Ireland

1. In the early 1900s, the Christian Church had a lot of influence in the UK. How do you think the Church's influence might have affected UK law on homosexuality?

_____

_____

_____

2. Why do you think some Christians and Muslims agreed with the legalisation of same-sex marriage in the UK? In your answer refer to specific religious beliefs.

Some Christians & muslims agree with it because they believe same sex marriages should not comit sinful acts (to have sex) and remain chaste.

_____

3. Why do you think some Christians and Muslims disagreed with the legalisation of same-sex marriage in the UK? In your answer, refer to specific religious beliefs.

_____

_____

_____

_____

Sources of religious belief and teaching

 Christianity: pages 68–69

For each of the quotations below, state whether you think it could be used to support or oppose homosexual relationships. Then briefly explain why. One example has been done for you.

Quotation	Does it support or oppose homosexual relationships?
❝If a man has sexual relations with a man as one does with a woman, both of them have done what is detestable.❞ *Leviticus* 20:13	*Oppose – because it says that if a man has sex with another man then they have both done something bad.*
❝That is why a man leaves his father and mother and is united to his wife, and they become one flesh.❞ *Genesis* 2:24	
❝To reject people on the grounds of their sexual orientation is a denial of God's creation.❞ *Towards a Quaker View of Sex, 1963*	
❝The proposition that same-sex relationships can embody crucial social values are not in dispute... Same-sex relationships often embody genuine mutuality and fidelity... The Church of England seeks to see those virtues maximised in society.❞ *The Church of England*	
❝There are absolutely no grounds for considering homosexual unions to be in any way similar or even remotely analogous to God's plan for marriage and family.❞ *Synod of Bishops, Catholic Church*	

Exam practice

Use your answers to the previous two activities to answer this exam question.

Give **two** religious beliefs about homosexuality. **[2 marks]**

1 _____

_____

2 _____

_____

Activity 1.2: Sex before marriage

 Christianity: page 70
Islam: page 58

Below are some different reasons to support or oppose sex before marriage. Number each one according to whether it is:

1. A Christian view to support sex before marriage

2. A Christian view to oppose sex before marriage

3. A Muslim view to oppose sex before marriage

If you think a view is held by both Christians *and* Muslims, then number it as '2' and '3'. An example has been done for you.

> TIP
>
> It is useful to know contrasting views about sex before marriage as you could be asked about these in the 4-mark question in your exam. (In Theme A you could also be asked about contrasting views on contraception and homosexual relationships.)

2 & 3
Sex is a gift from God and should be treated seriously

Sex before marriage can be a valid expression of a couple's love for each other

Paul called for sexual restraint when he wrote 'Flee from sexual immorality' (*1 Corinthians* 6:180)

Sex before marriage is an offense in Shari'ah law

Sex should be part of the loving, trusting relationship developed within marriage

The Catholic Church teaches that unmarried people should not have sex

Exam practice

Use your answers to Activity 1.2 to answer this exam question.

Explain **two** contrasting religious beliefs about sexual relationships before marriage.

In your answer you must refer to one or more religious traditions.

[4 marks]

_____

_____

_____

_____

_____

_____

_____

_____

_____

_____

_____

TIP

While you do not need to refer to a source of religious belief and teaching in a 4-mark question, you are allowed to and it can often make your answer more relevant and developed.

Key terms

 Christianity: pages 68–83
Islam: pages 56–71

Some key terms are very similar, so it is important to know what the difference is between them. Carefully define each key term below to make sure you can distinguish between them.

TIP

It's important to know the definitions of key terms. This will help you to understand the questions in the exam, and also to write better answers.

Key term 1	Key term 2
Heterosexual	Homosexual

Key term 1	Key term 2
Sex before marriage	Sex outside of marriage
Cohabitation	Marriage
Divorce	Remarriage
Nuclear family	Extended family
Gender prejudice	Gender discrimination
Civil partnership	Same-sex marriage

Sources of religious belief and teaching

 Christianity: pages 72–73
Islam: pages 60–61

Answer the following questions about sources of religious belief and teaching linked to contraception.

1. *Humanae Vitae* says that 'Every sexual act should have the possibility of creating new life.'
   Which Christian denomination do you think agrees with this belief? Give reasons for your answer.

   _____

   _____

   _____

   _____

2. **The Lambeth Conference agreed that artificial contraception could be used 'in the light of Christian principles.'**
   What do you think this means?

   _____

   _____

   _____

   _____

   _____

3. **In Genesis, God tells Adam and Eve to 'be fruitful and increase in number.'**
   Why do some Christians use this as an argument to oppose the use of contraception?

   _____

   _____

   _____

   _____

   _____

4. **Some Muslims use *Qur'an* 4:28 to justify the use of contraception as it says 'God wishes to lighten your burden.'**
   Explain what 'burden' means here and how using contraception would 'lighten' it.

   _____

   _____

   _____

   _____

   _____

5. ***Qur'an* 17:31 says 'Do not kill your children for fear of poverty – we shall provide for them and for you.'**
   Do you think this quotation could be used to support or oppose the use of contraception? Explain your answer.

   _____

   _____

   _____

   _____

Activity 1.3: Answering an exam question on contraception

 Christianity: pages 72–73
Islam: pages 60–61

Two students have written an answer to the following exam question:

Explain **two** contrasting religious beliefs about contraception.

In your answer you must refer to one or more religious traditions.   **[4 marks]**

Read each of the answers below. Identify what each student has done well and what they could do to improve their work.

> **TIP**
>
> When reading each answer, think about the following:
> - Is it factually correct and does it make sense?
> - Has the student made good use of key terms?
> - Has the student added detail or explanation to their points?
> - Are the religious beliefs contrasting (different)?

Student 1

Some Christians don't allow the use of contraception as they believe that it stops procreation which is the purpose of sex. 'Be fruitful and multiply.'

Some Muslims also don't allow the use of contraception as they believe the purpose of marriage is to have children.

What they've done well	What they can do to improve their answer

Student 2

Some Christians don't allow the use of contraception as they believe that it stops procreation which is the purpose of sex. They believe that one of the Ten Commandments is 'be fruitful and multiply'.

Other Christians allow the use of contraception as they believe that all children should be brought in to a loving and well supported family. By using contraception a couple can make sure they are emotionally and financially ready for it.

What they've done well	What they can do to improve their answer

Activity 1.4: Christian wedding vows

S B   **Christianity: pages 74–75**

A Here is an example of a Christian wedding vow. In the space provided, explain what the lines in bold mean. How do they reflect Christian teachings about what is important in a marriage? One example is given for you.

I, [name], take you, [name],

to be my husband/wife,

to have and to hold ——————— Physical intimacy is an important part of marriage. This is also emphasised in Genesis when it says that a husband and wife 'become one flesh'.

from this day forward;

for better, for worse, ———————

for richer, for poorer,

in sickness and in health,

to love and to cherish, ———————

till death us do part; ———————

according to God's holy law.

In the presence of God I make this vow. ———————

B What does this wedding vow tell you about the importance of marriage in Christianity?

_____

_____

_____

_____

Activity 1.5: Reasons for divorce

 Christianity: page 76

Look at the reasons for divorce below and then answer the following questions.

1. Some Christians think divorce is acceptable in certain situations. Which of the reasons above do you think Christians would be **least** likely to agree is a valid reason for divorce? Explain your answer.

_____

_____

_____

_____

2. Which of the reasons above do you think Christians would be **most** likely to agree is a valid reason for divorce? Explain your answer.

_____

_____

_____

_____

3. Do you think that all of the reasons are valid reasons for divorce? Explain your answer.

_____

_____

_____

_____

Activity 1.6: Religious teachings about divorce and remarriage

 Christianity: pages 76–77
Islam: pages 64–65

A The following table gives some arguments to support and oppose divorce and remarriage. Add **one** more argument to each column in the table, you might want to add a specific reference to religious teachings. For example, *Mark* 10:9 or *Qur'an* 4:35 could be useful when thinking about divorce and remarriage.

Arguments to support divorce and remarriage	Arguments to oppose divorce and remarriage
Jesus taught that compassion and love are important; in some cases divorce may be more compassionate	The wedding vows made before God are sacred and cannot be broken
The Church should reflect the forgiveness of God and allow people to find happiness in a second marriage	If people are allowed to divorce then they won't take marriage seriously
The Prophet Muhammad married a divorced woman	In the Bible, Jesus taught that anyone who divorces and remarries is committing adultery

B Now answer the following questions.

1. Which of the arguments above do you think is one of the strongest? Explain why.

_____

_____

_____

2. Which of the arguments above do you think is one of the weakest? Explain why.

_____

_____

_____

TIP

You might consider an argument to be strong if it is supported by a core religious belief or teaching. You might consider an argument to be weak if it is just a personal opinion, there is no strong evidence to support it, or it only applies in some situations.

3. Overall, do you think religious believers should support divorce and remarriage? Explain why.

_____

_____

_____

_____

Exam practice

Use your answers to the previous two activities to help you write an answer to this exam question.

'No one should be allowed to divorce and remarry.'

Evaluate this statement.

In your answer you:

- should give reasoned arguments in support of this statement
- should give reasoned arguments to support a different point of view
- should refer to religious arguments
- may refer to non-religious arguments
- should reach a justified conclusion.

[12 marks]
[SPaG 3 marks]

TIP

In a 12-mark question, use the bullet points given in the question as a checklist to check that you have included everything needed.

Aim to write at least three paragraphs in a 12-mark question:

1) arguments to support the statement
2) arguments supporting a different view
3) a justified conclusion.

Key terms

Christianity: pages 68–83
Islam: pages 56–71

For each of the statements below, identify which key term could be used instead of the text written in bold and then write the word or phrase in the box provided.

TIP

In your exam you can assume that the examiner will know the meanings of key religious terms, so you don't need to waste time explaining what they mean.

1. Some Christians think it is acceptable for people to **live together before they marry**, as long as they are in a faithful and loving relationship that will lead to marriage.

Key term	

2. Some Muslims are against using **something to stop a woman getting pregnant**, as they believe that God gives people strength to cope with any children.

Key term	

3. Christians accept relationships that are **between a man and a woman**, but some Christians do not agree with relationships that are **between two people of the same sex**, as the Bible says this is a sin.

Key term 1	
Key term 2	

4. Catholic Christians do not believe in **a person getting married again while their former husband or wife is still alive**, as they believe that marriage is until death and divorce is not allowed.

Key term	

5. Many Christians believe in **both genders being given the same rights and opportunities as each other**, as God created all humans in his image.

Key term	

6. Muslims believe that **having babies** is important, as children are a blessing from God and this allows Islam to continue into the next generation.

Key term	

Activity 1.7: Family types

 Christianity: pages 78–79
Islam: pages 66–67

There are many different types of family. Look at the pictures below and write in the left-hand column which type of family each one is. Then, in the right-hand column of the table, give a religious attitude or teaching towards this type of family. The first one has been done for you.

single-parent family   nuclear family   extended family   same-sex parents   step-family

	Type of family	Religious attitude or teaching towards this type of family
	Single-parent family	Christian churches acknowledge that there are many reasons why single-parent families exist, and they try to help single parents by providing childcare or other support.

Exam practice

Use your answers to the previous activity to answer this exam question.

Which **one** of the following best describes a family with children, parents and grandparents living together?   **[1 mark]**

A Extended family

B Nuclear family

C Step-family

D Single-parent family

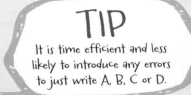

TIP

It is time efficient and less likely to introduce any errors to just write A, B, C or D.

Activity 1.8: The purpose of families

 Christianity: pages 80–81
Islam: pages 68–69

Three purposes of the family are given below. Explain why each of these purposes are important to religious believers. Try to support your explanation with a religious teaching, belief or quotation.

Purpose of the family	Why is this important to religious believers?
Bringing children into the world	
To educate children about the faith	
To provide safety and security for the sick, elderly and disabled	

Sources of religious belief and teaching

Christianity: pages 68–83
Islam: pages 56–71

For each of the topics in the table below, think of a short quotation that could be used to represent a Christian view on it, and another quotation that could be used to support a Muslim view. Make sure you give the source of the quotation as well (although you don't need to give an exact reference). One example has been completed for you.

> ## TIP
>
> A sacred text (such as the Bible or the Qur'an) is an obvious source of religious quotations, but you could also refer to other texts (such as set prayers and creeds), or official statements from a religious group or leader (such as from the Catholic Church or an Imam).

	Christianity	Islam
Homosexual relationships		
Sex before marriage	'Your body is the temple of the Holy Spirit' – the Bible	
Contraception		
Marriage		

Divorce		
Families		
Roles of men and women		

Exam practice

Use your answers to the previous two activities to help you answer this exam question.

Explain **two** religious beliefs about the purpose of families.

Refer to sacred writings or another source of religious belief and teaching in your answer.

[5 marks]

_____

_____

_____

_____

_____

_____

_____

TIP

Remember that the 'purpose of families' means what families are for, or why families are needed in society.

_____
_____
_____
_____
_____
_____

Activity 1.9: Gender equality in the UK

Christianity: pages 82–83

Look at this timeline showing some laws related to gender equality in the UK from the past century. Then answer the questions below.

1918 The Parliament Act – allowed women to become MPs

1928 Equal Franchise Act – gave women the same voting rights as men

1967 Family Planning Act – made contraception easily available through the NHS

1970 Equal Pay Act – meant men and women should be paid equally for doing the same work

1975 The Sex Discrimination Act – made gender discrimination illegal

1. Which of these laws do you think might have had the most impact on reducing gender discrimination in the UK? Explain your choice.

_____
_____
_____
_____
_____
_____

2. Which of these laws do you think some Christians might disapprove of? Explain your choice.

_____
_____
_____
_____
_____

Challenge activity 1.10: Muhammad's final sermon

 Islam: pages 70–71

This is part of the Prophet Muhammad's final sermon before he died:

> "O People, it is true that you have certain rights with regard to your women, but they also have rights over you. Remember that you have taken them as your wives only under a trust from God and with His permission. If they abide by your right then to them belongs the right to be fed and clothed in kindness. Do treat your women well and be kind to them for they are your partners and committed helpers. And it is your right that they do not make friends with any one of whom you do not approve, as well as never to be unchaste."

A Why do you think Muhammad included this in his final sermon?

_____

_____

_____

_____

B How might Muhammad's words influence Muslims today?

_____

_____

_____

_____

C It is often said that in Islam women and men are 'equal but have different roles'. What does this mean?

_____

_____

_____

_____

D Do you think Muhammad is supporting gender equality or not? Give reasons for your answer.

_____

_____

_____

Key Terms Glossary

As you progress through the course, you can collect the meanings of useful terms in the glossary below. You can then use the completed glossaries to revise from.

To do well in the exam you will need to understand these terms and include them in your answers. Tick the shaded circles to record how confident you feel.

Family

- ○ **I recognise this term**
- ◔ **I understand what this term means**
- ● **I can use this term in a sentence**

Cohabitation

Family planning

Contraception

Gender discrimination

Divorce

Gender equality

Educating children in a faith

Gender prejudice

Extended family

Heterosexual

Homosexual _____
_____
_____
_____
_____
_____

Protection of children _____
_____
_____
_____
_____
_____

Human sexuality _____
_____
_____
_____
_____
_____

Remarriage _____
_____
_____
_____
_____
_____

Marriage _____
_____
_____
_____
_____
_____

Same-sex marriage _____
_____
_____
_____
_____
_____

Nuclear family _____
_____
_____
_____
_____
_____

Same-sex parents _____
_____
_____
_____
_____
_____

Polygamy _____
_____
_____
_____
_____
_____

Sex before marriage _____
_____
_____
_____
_____
_____

Procreation _____
_____
_____
_____
_____
_____

Sex outside of marriage _____
_____
_____
_____
_____
_____

Chapter 2: Theme B: Religion and life

Activity 2.1: The origins of the universe

Christianity: pages 86–87
Islam: pages 74–75

Answer these questions about the origins of the universe.

1. Briefly summarise the Big Bang Theory.

   The Big Bang theory is an event that includes a meteor

2. Summarise how Christians believe the universe began.

3. Summarise how Muslims believe the universe began.

4. Explain how a religious teaching could support the Big Bang Theory.

5. Explain how a religious teaching could oppose the Big Bang Theory.

Key terms

 Christianity: pages 88–89
Islam: pages 76–77

A Match up these three key terms to the correct definitions in the table below:

Dominion	Stewardship	Responsibility

Key term	Definition
	The idea that believers have a duty to look after the environment on behalf of God
	The idea that believers have the power and authority to rule over God's creation
	Having a duty to do something or take care of something

B For each key term, write a sentence to explain what Christians or Muslims believe about it in relation to looking after the world. Use the key term in your sentence.

Dominion:

_____

_____

_____

Stewardship:

_____

_____

_____

Responsibility:

_____

_____

_____

> **TIP**
>
> An example sentence might be: 'The Qur'an says that God gave humans the **responsibility** of looking after the earth.' Now try to come up with three sentences of your own.

Exam practice

Now answer the following question.

Which **one** of the following means having the authority to rule over the earth? **[1 mark]**

A Awe

B Dominion

C Stewardship

D Responsibility

_____

Activity 2.2: The value of the world

 Christianity: pages 88–89
Islam: pages 76–77

Answer the following questions about valuing the world.

1. What is the role of khalifahs?

_____

_____

_____

_____

2. Explain how Christians and Muslims have similar views about dominion.

_____

_____

_____

_____

_____

3. Give **two** examples of how humans might experience awe and wonder in the natural world.

_____

_____

_____

_____

_____

4. Give **two** ways that people could show responsibility for looking after the earth.

_____

_____

_____

_____

_____

5. For religious believers, give **two** consequences of not looking after the earth.

_____

_____

_____

_____

_____

Activity 2.3: The use and abuse of the environment

Christianity: pages 90–91
Islam: pages 78–79

A Fill in the table below with three more examples of threats to the environment. Then in the right-hand column, add one way that Christians and Muslims can help to combat each of these threats.

Threats to the environment	An action Christians or Muslims could take to help tackle this problem
Deforestation	Buy from companies that plant trees to replace the trees they have used

B Three religious quotations are given below. Explain how each quotation can be used to argue that it is important to look after the environment.

Quotation	How does this quotation show it is important to look after the environment?
❝The earth is the Lord's and everything in it.❞ *Psalm* 24:1	*This quotation means that our planet was made by and owned by God. This means we should look after it as it isn't ours to pollute and destroy.*
❝The Lord God took the man and put him in the Garden of Eden to work it and take care of it.❞ *Genesis* 2:15	
❝Do not seek from it more than what you need.❞ *Hadith*	

Exam practice

Use your answers to Activity 2.3 to answer this exam question.

Give **two** ways that religious believers can help to protect the environment. **[2 marks]**

1 _____

_____

2 _____

_____

Activity 2.4: The use and abuse of animals

Christianity: pages 94–95
Islam: pages 80–81

Complete the table below to show the views that Christians or Muslims might have on the different ways in which animals are used. Then for each view, give a reason for it. One has been done for you.

TIP

When giving a reason for a view, think about the religious belief or teaching that might support the view. If you can, use a quotation to help explain the reason.

Use	Christian or Muslim view	Reason
Keeping animals in zoos	Some Muslims would be against zoos as animals are kept in cages.	Muslims believe animals are valuable to God and should be treated with kindness and compassion. Some cages are too small for the animals to be treated as they should be, which isn't kind.
Using animals for transport		

Use	Christian or Muslim view	Reason
Using animals for food		
Hunting animals for entertainment		
Experimenting on animals to test medicines		
Experimenting on animals to test cosmetics		

Activity 2.5: The origins of human life in the Bible and the Qur'an

 Christianity: pages 96–97
Islam: pages 82–83

Christians and Muslims have some similar views about the origins of human life, based on the story of Adam and Eve in the Bible and the Qur'an. There are also a few differences in the details of the story.

Decide if each of the beliefs in the boxes below is considered to be Christian or Muslim or both.

- If you think it is a Muslim belief, write 'M' in the circle.

- If you think it is a Christian belief, write 'C' in the circle.

- If you think it is both a Christian and Muslim belief, write 'M' and 'C'.

One has been done for you.

M & C — God named the first human being Adam

While Adam was sleeping, God took one of his ribs and formed Eve, the first woman

Adam and Eve were banished from the Garden of Eden by God

The whole human race is descended from Adam and Eve

Adam and Eve were tempted to eat the forbidden fruit

God formed the first human from the ground and breathed life into him

God created Adam's wife, Eve (Hawwa), from the same soul

God sent Adam and Eve down to earth from paradise in order to start a human world

Activity 2.6: Religious views on the theory of evolution

 Christianity: pages 96–97
Islam: pages 82–83

Answer these questions about the theory of evolution.

1. In one sentence, give a summary of the theory of evolution.

_____

_____

2. Some Christians and Muslims reject the theory of evolution. Why is this?

_____

_____

_____

_____

3. Why do some Christians and Muslims believe it is possible to accept the theory of evolution and still believe in God?

_____

_____

_____

_____

_____

Exam practice

Use your answers to the previous two activities to help answer this exam question.

Explain **two** similar religious beliefs about the origins of human life.

In your answer you must refer to one or more religious traditions.

[4 marks]

_____

_____

_____

_____

_____

_____

_____

_____

TIP

Always read the question carefully. An important word here is 'similar'. For example, you could give a similar Christian belief and Muslim belief about how God created human life.

Activity 2.7: Christian views on abortion

 Christianity: pages 98–99

Christians have different views on abortion. They may use the following Bible verses to help them decide if it is acceptable or not.

In the table below, decide if each argument could be used to support or oppose abortion, by writing 'for' or 'against' in the middle column. Then, decide which of the quotations could be used to support each argument. Write the relevant number in the last column of the table. An example has been done for you.

1. **"** 'Love your neighbour as yourself.' There is no commandment greater than these. **"**
   Mark 12:31

2. **"** So God created mankind in his own image. **"**
   Genesis 1:27

3. **"** You shall not murder. **"**
   Exodus 20:13

4. **"** Repent, then, and turn to God, so that your sins may be wiped out, that times of refreshing may come from the Lord. **"**
   Acts 3:19

5. **"** Before I formed you in the womb I knew you, before you were born I set you apart. **"**
   Jeremiah 1:5

6. **"** Do you not know that your bodies are temples of the Holy Spirit, who is in you, whom you have received from God? You are not your own. **"**
   1 Corinthians 6:19

Argument	For/against abortion?	Quotation that supports this view
It is taking a life so a type of murder	*Against*	3
Only God should decide what happens with our bodies		
God creates life so only God can take it away		
God forgives us when we have to do something to get out of a bad situation		
God has already planned a person's life before they are born		
Sometimes it might be the most loving thing for the mother or the baby		

Activity 2.8: Muslim views on abortion

 Islam: pages 84–85

In the first column of the table below, explain what each key term means. Then, in the second column, explain how this key term affects Muslim attitudes towards abortion.

Key term	What does this term mean?	How does it influence Muslim views about abortion?
Sanctity of life		
Quality of life		
Ensoulment		

Exam practice

Use your answers to the previous two activities to answer this exam practice question.

Explain **two** religious beliefs about abortion.

Refer to sacred writings or another source of religious belief and teaching in your answer.　　　**[5 marks]**

_____

_____

_____

_____

_____

_____

_____

_____

_____

_____

_____

Activity 2.9: Arguments for and against euthanasia

 Christianity: pages 100–101
Islam: pages 86–87

Most Christians and Muslims are against euthanasia. Read these arguments for and against euthanasia and then answer the questions below.

 A God gives life and only God should take life

B God gave people free will so they should be able to choose what to do with their lives

C Euthanasia would change the role of doctors from saving lives to also taking lives

 D God has planned our lives and euthanasia might be going against his plan

 E Life is a gift from God so it should always be valued

F People might abuse the system and kill people who aren't really suffering for their own benefit

 G Hospices can care for those who are dying with dignity and with as little pain as possible

 H God gave us knowledge of painkillers so we should use these instead of killing someone

I Euthanasia is murder

1. Which of these arguments might a Muslim consider to be one of the most important reasons to oppose euthanasia? Explain your answer.

_____

_____

_____

2. Do you think that argument D is a strong or weak argument? Explain your answer.

_____

_____

_____

3. Which passage from the Bible might a Christian use to support argument I?

_____

_____

4. Which argument might a Christian use to support euthanasia?

_____

5. Give **one** more argument, not suggested above, that a Christian might use to support euthanasia.

_____

_____

_____

Activity 2.10: Answering an exam question on euthanasia

  Christianity: pages 100–101
Islam: pages 86–87

Three students have written an answer to the following exam question:

Explain **two** contrasting religious beliefs about euthanasia.

In your answer you must refer to one or more religious traditions.   **[4 marks]**

Read each of the answers below. Identify what each student has done well and what they could do to improve their work.

> TIP
>
> When reading each answer, think about the following:
> • Is it factually correct and does it make sense?
> • Has the student made good use of key terms?
> • Has the student added detail or explanation to their points?
> • Are the religious beliefs contrasting (different)?

Student 1

Some religious people believe that it is OK. Others don't think it should be allowed.

What they've done well	What they can do to improve their answer

Student 2

Some Christians believe that it is acceptable in some circumstances, as it would be the most loving thing for the mother. They believe that God is omniscient so knows the situation that a woman might be in, and is also omnibenevolent so he wouldn't want her to suffer if she carried on with the pregnancy.

Most Christians are against it as they believe it goes against the sanctity of life.

What they've done well	What they can do to improve their answer

Student 3

Some Christians believe it is not acceptable as it goes against God's plan for a person. They believe that God gives life and only God should decide when to take life away.

Most Muslims are also against it as they also believe that it is only Allah who should take life. If someone takes another person's life then they are 'playing God' which is shirk, the worst sin. The Qur'an says 'God wishes to lighten your burden; man was created weak.'

What they've done well	What they can do to improve their answer

Activity 2.11: Beliefs about the afterlife

 Christianity: pages 102–103
Islam: pages 88–89

Christians and Muslims have some similar views about the afterlife. There are also a few differences in the details.

Decide if each of the beliefs below is considered to be Christian or Muslim or both.

- If you think it is a Muslim belief, write 'M' in the circle.
- If you think it is a Christian belief, write 'C'.
- If you think it is both a Christian and Muslim belief, write 'M' and 'C'.

One has been done for you.

M

There is a state of waiting after death called 'barzakh'

Our bodies will be resurrected on Judgement Day

People who are judged favourably by God will enter heaven (Jannah)

People are judged by God on the Day of Judgement

People are judged by God as soon as they die

Some people's souls are cleansed in Purgatory

Challenge activity 2.12: Why does a person go to heaven or hell?

 Christianity: pages 102–103
Islam: pages 88–89

Read this text and then answer the questions that follow.

In the Parable of the Rich Man and Lazarus (*Luke* 16:19-31), a rich man never helps or pays attention to the poor, homeless man who sits outside the gates to his house. When both men die, the rich man goes to hell and the poor man goes to heaven.

In the Parable of the Sheep and Goats (*Matthew* 25:31-46), Jesus tells his followers that when they help people in need, it is as if they are helping Jesus himself.

James 4:17 says that 'If anyone, then, knows the good they ought to do and doesn't do it, it is sin for them.'

A What do these teachings suggest about the effect a person's actions have on whether they go to heaven or hell? Explain your answer.

_____

_____

_____

_____

B Why do some Christians believe that doing good actions is not enough by itself to earn a place in heaven?

_____

_____

_____

C A minority of Christians believe that everyone will go to heaven regardless of how they live their lives. Which event in Christian history makes this possible?

_____

D For Muslims, how does the idea of free will influence what happens in the afterlife?

_____

_____

_____

_____

E For Muslims, why do you think doing good deeds in their lifetime is important? Explain your answer.

_____

_____

_____

Exam practice

Use your answers to the previous two activities to write a complete answer to this exam question.

'Our actions determine if we go to heaven or hell.'

Evaluate this statement.

In your answer you:

- should give reasoned arguments in support of this statement
- should give reasoned arguments to support a different point of view
- should refer to religious arguments
- may refer to non-religious arguments
- should reach a justified conclusion.

[12 marks]
[SPaG 3 marks]

TIP

Your SPaG will be assessed in 12-mark questions so read through your answer carefully and check you've:
- Used the spellings given in the statement
- Shown clear paragraphs
- Used relevant key words.

Key terms

 Christianity: pages 86–103
Islam: pages 74–89

Some key terms are very similar, so it is important to know what the difference is between them. Carefully define each key term below to make sure you can distinguish between them.

Key term 1	Key term 2
The origins of the universe	The origins of life
Dominion	Stewardship
Natural resources	Renewable resources
Vegan	Vegetarian
Sanctity of life	Quality of life
Abortion	Euthanasia
Voluntary euthanasia	Non-voluntary euthanasia

Sources of religious belief and teaching

 Christianity: pages 86–103
Islam: pages 74–89

A   Look at these quotations from the Bible and the Qur'an.

> "Those whose good deeds weigh heavy will be successful."
>
> *Qur'an* 23:102

> "Depart from me, you who are cursed, into the eternal fire prepared for the devil and his angels."
>
> *Matthew* 25:41

> "Then the LORD God formed a man from the dust of the ground and breath into his nostrils the breath of life."
>
> *Genesis* 2:7

> "Whoever kills a sparrow or anything bigger than that without a just cause, God will hold him accountable on the Day of Judgement."
>
> *Hadith*

> "Everything that lives and moves about will be food for you."
>
> *Genesis* 9:3

> "Before I formed you in the womb I knew you, before you were born I set you apart."
>
> *Jeremiah* 1:5

> "You shall not murder."
>
> *Exodus* 20:13

> "You [humans] were lifeless and He gave you life."
>
> *Qur'an* 2:28

> "Do not kill each other, for God is merciful to you."
>
> *Qur'an* 4:29

> "Do not kill your children for fear of poverty – We shall provide for them and for you – killing them is a great sin."
>
> *Qur'an* 17:31

B   For each of the topics below, decide which of the quotations above could be used to represent a Christian or Muslim view about it. Use each quotation once only. One has been done for you as an example.

Abortion:

Christian	Muslim
'Before I formed you in the womb I knew you, before you were born I set you apart.' Jeremiah 1:5	

Euthanasia:

Christian	Muslim

Life after death:

Christian	Muslim

The origins of life:

Christian	Muslim

The use of animals:

Christian	Muslim

Key Terms Glossary

As you progress through the course, you can collect the meanings of useful terms in the glossary below. You can then use the completed glossaries to revise from.

To do well in the exam you will need to understand these terms and include them in your answers. Tick the shaded

circles to record how confident you feel. Use the extra boxes at the end to record any other terms that you have found difficult, along with their definitions.

○ **I recognise this term**

◐ **I understand what this term means**

● **I can use this term in a sentence**

Abortion

Abuse

Afterlife

Animal experimentation

Awe

Big Bang theory

Dominion

Environment

Euthanasia

Evolution

Natural resources

Origins of life _____

_____

_____

_____

_____

Stewardship _____

_____

_____

_____

_____

Origins of the universe _____

_____

_____

_____

_____

Universe _____

_____

_____

_____

_____

Pollution _____

_____

_____

_____

_____

Wonder _____

_____

_____

_____

_____

Quality of life _____

_____

_____

_____

_____

_____

_____

_____

_____

_____

Responsibility _____

_____

_____

_____

_____

_____

_____

_____

_____

_____

Sanctity of life _____

_____

_____

_____

_____

_____

_____

_____

_____

_____

Chapter 3: **Theme C: The existence of God and revelation**

Activity 3.1: The Design argument

 Christianity: pages 106–107
Islam: pages 92–93

The following ideas have been put forward by philosophers to argue that God designed the universe.

In the first column of the table, explain how each idea can be used to show that God designed the universe. Then in the second column of the table, explain how an atheist might respond. Try to use examples to support your explanation where appropriate.

 TIP
Remember the important key terms here: a 'theist' is someone who believes in God and an 'atheist' is someone who believes there is no God.

Idea	Theist explanation	Atheist response
The universe is in a regular order		
Humans have thumbs		
There is evidence of design in the natural world		
Everything is just right for human life to develop		

Activity 3.2: Objections to the Design argument

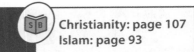

Christianity: page 107
Islam: page 93

For each of the objections to the Design argument given below, explain how a theist might respond.

Objection	Theist response
An all-loving God would not allow humans to suffer as much as they do	
Some of God's design seems to be flawed	
The theory of evolution suggests that species have developed by chance, not because of a designer God	

Exam practice

Now answer the following exam question.

Which **one** of the following is the argument that God designed the universe because everything in nature is too intricate and complex to have happened by chance?   **[1 mark]**

A   The Design argument

B   The First Cause argument

C   Atheism

D   Creationism

Activity 3.3: The First Cause argument

Christianity: pages 108–109
Islam: pages 94–95

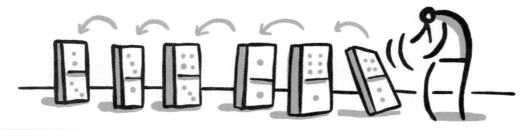

A Number the boxes from 1 to 5 to put the different parts of the First Cause argument into a logical order. ('1' should be the first part of the argument and '5' should be the last.)

There had to be something eternal that was not caused by anything

Therefore God exists

Everything that exists or begins to exist must have a cause

The eternal first cause is God

The universe exists and began to exist, so it too must have a cause

B Choose **two** parts of the argument and explain how they might be considered to be weak. Think about how you would argue against these parts of the First Cause argument.

Part of the argument	Weakness

Activity 3.4: The argument from miracles

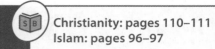

Christianity: pages 110–111
Islam: pages 96–97

Answer the following questions about miracles.

1. What is a miracle?

_____

_____

_____

2. Why do some theists think miracles are proof that God exists?

_____

_____

_____

3. What is the 'supreme miracle' in Islam?

_____

_____

4. Why is this miracle so important to Muslims?

_____

_____

_____

5. Name **two** important miracles in Christianity.

_____

_____

6. The Catholic Church has recognised 69 miracles as having taken place in Lourdes. These are usually events where people with a serious illness have got better after visiting. What criteria might have been used to confirm if these events were miracles or not?

_____

_____

_____

_____

_____

TIP

Think about the arguments for and against these events being a miracle. Why might a person have got better? What reasons would you want to rule out before deciding it was the work of God?

Activity 3.5: Answering an exam question on miracles

Christianity: pages 110–111
Islam: pages 96–97

Three students have written an answer to the following exam question:

Explain **two** contrasting beliefs in contemporary British society about miracles.

In your answer you should refer to the main religious tradition of Great Britain and non-religious beliefs. **[4 marks]**

Read each of the answers below. Identify what each student has done well and what they could do to improve their work.

TIP

When reading each answer, think about the following:
- Is it factually correct and does it make sense?
- Has the student made good use of key terms?
- Has the student added detail or explanation to their points?
- Has the student referred to the main religious tradition of Great Britain and non-religious beliefs?
- Are the beliefs contrasting (different)?

Student 1

Christians believe that Jesus performed miracles.

I don't believe that he did as they are just stories that are made up in the Bible.

What they've done well	What they can do to improve their answer

Student 2

Most Muslims believe that some people have had significant religious experiences that might be called miracles. For example, when Muhammad ascended to heaven.

Other Muslims would say that the supreme miracle within Islam is the revelation of the Qur'an to Muhammad. Muslims believe that only Allah could write such a book; no human could.

What they've done well	What they can do to improve their answer

Student 3

Miracles are very important in Christianity. Jesus performed many miracles. Some of his famous miracles that can be read in the Bible show us that he was the Son of God, as he had the power to do things such as walk on water, bring people back from the dead and heal sick people. There are so many things that he did that normal humans can't do. Some Christians think the ultimate miracle is Jesus dying on the cross and resurrecting on the third day. We know that humans can't come back to life once they have died so this is a very convincing miracle.

What they've done well	What they can do to improve their answer

Activity 3.6: The miracle of Muhammad's ascent into heaven

S B Islam: page 97

Read about Muhammad's ascent into heaven (al-Mi'raj) and answer the following questions.

1. Who woke Muhammad up?

_____

2. What did the strange angelic beast look like?

_____

_____

3. To which city was Muhammad first taken?

_____

4. How was Muhammad tested?

_____

_____

_____

_____

5. Where was the 'ascent' to?

_____

6. How many times did God initially tell Muslims to pray?

_____

7. Which other prophet did Muhammad meet on the way back?

_____

8. Why do you think this prophet asked Muhammad to try to reduce the number of prayers?

_____

_____

Activity 3.7: Further arguments against the existence of God   Christianity: pages 112–113
Islam: pages 98–99

TIP
If you think a theist could use the Bible or Qur'an to support their response, say which bit of the Bible or Qur'an in particular.

Answer the following questions about arguments against the existence of God. Try to refer to both Christianity and Islam in your answers.

Science
Why do some people think that science proves God does not exist?

_____

_____

_____

How might a theist respond to these arguments?

_____

_____

_____

Give **one** source of religious belief and teaching that a theist could use to support their response.

_____

_____

Evil and suffering

Why do some people think that evil and suffering prove God does not exist?

_____

_____

_____

_____

How might a theist respond to these arguments?

_____

_____

_____

_____

Give **one** source of religious belief and teaching that a theist could use to support their response.

_____

_____

_____

Exam practice

Use your answers to the previous activity to help you answer this exam question.

Explain **two** religious beliefs about the existence of evil and suffering in the world.

Refer to sacred writings or another source of religious belief and teaching in your answer.   **[5 marks]**

_____

_____

_____

_____

_____

_____

_____

_____

_____

TIP

Your answer could explain why believers think evil and suffering exist, or how believers think they should respond to evil and suffering. Both beliefs could come from one religion or you could refer to two different religions.

Activity 3.8: Special revelation and general revelation

Christianity: pages 114–117
Islam: pages 100–103

A According to Christianity, which of the following are examples of special revelation and which are examples of general revelation?

	Special	General
The Pope giving Catholics guidance	☐	☐
Receiving a prophecy from an angel	☐	☐
Seeing Jesus during a near-death experience	☐	☐
Praying to God	☐	☐
Experiencing a healing miracle	☐	☐
Reading the Bible	☐	☐
Looking at stars in the night sky and realising how powerful God is	☐	☐

B Answer the following questions about special revelation in Islam.

1. Muslims believe that divine revelations are only received by prophets and messengers. Why does this mean that special revelation is not something that can be experienced by Muslims today?

_____

_____

_____

2. Do Muslims believe that visions are a type of special revelation? Why or why not?

_____

_____

_____

Exam practice

Now answer the following exam question.

Give **two** types of special revelation.   **[2 marks]**

1 _____

_____

2 _____

_____

Activity 3.9: Visions in Christianity

 Christianity: page 115

Answer the following questions about visions in Christianity.

1. What is a vision?

_____

_____

2. Describe **one** example of a vision in Christianity. Who saw the vision? What did they see? How did it change them?

_____

_____

_____

_____

> **TIP**
>
> Try to remember this example for your exam, as you may be asked to write about it.

3. What questions do you think could be asked to test whether a vision is 'real' or not?

_____

_____

_____

_____

4. A woman is weak from an operation and hasn't eaten for 12 hours. While lying in her hospital bed she sees a vision of Jesus, who tells her that the key to a successful life is to generate great wealth. The woman recovers and spends the rest of her life dedicated to her work as an accountant, eventually becoming very wealthy.

Do you think Christians would view this as a genuine vision? Why or why not?

_____

_____

_____

_____

5. What alternative explanation might an atheist give for why some people see 'visions'?

_____

_____

_____

Activity 3.10: Nature and scripture as a way of understanding the divine

 Christianity: pages 116–117
Islam: pages 102–103

Answer the following questions about understanding the divine through nature and scripture.

1. Christians and Muslims believe that God is powerful, creative, intelligent, benevolent and awesome. How do things in nature help to illustrate these characteristics? One example is given below. Pick another **two** characteristics and give an example for each.

Characteristic	Example in nature
Powerful	Hurricanes and storms demonstrate the power of God.

2. Christians and Muslims believe that observing nature can teach them about God. What do humanists believe can be learned from observing nature?

_____

_____

_____

3. Christians believe the Bible tells them the following three things about God. For each one, explain why it is important for Christians today.

	Why is knowing this important for Christians today?
What God is like	
How God acted in the past	
How God wants people to live today	

4. Why is the Qur'an so important to Muslims in helping them to understand the divine?

_____

_____

_____

_____

Exam practice

Use your answers to the previous activity to help you answer this exam question.

Explain **two** contrasting beliefs in contemporary British society about nature as a way of understanding the divine.

In your answer you should refer to the main religious tradition of Great Britain and non-religious beliefs. **[4 marks]**

_____

_____

_____

_____

_____

_____

_____

_____

_____

_____

TIP

Remember that the 'main religious tradition of Great Britain' is Christianity, so here you need to give one Christian belief about nature as general revelation and a different atheist or humanist belief about nature as general revelation.

Challenge activity 3.11: The 99 names of Allah

 Islam: pages 104–105

In Islam there are 99 names for God. Fifteen of these names are given here.

1. The All Mighty	6. The Watchful	11. The Hidden
2. The Creator	7. The Loving	12. The Eternal Ruler
3. The All Knowing	8. The Protecting Friend	13. The Guide
4. The Most Just	9. The Giver of Life	14. The Incomparable
5. The Generous One	10. The Powerful	15. The Avenger

A The table below gives five of God's characteristics. For each of the characteristics, pick two of the names above that you think best describe that characteristic. Then in the right hand column, give a reason for one of your choices. One has been done for you as an example.

Characteristic	Name	Reason for one of your choices
Omnipotent	1 *The Powerful* 2 *The All Mighty*	*Omnipotent means having unlimited power. 'The Powerful' suggests God has a lot of power.*

Characteristic	Name	Reason for one of your choices
Immanent	1 _____ _____ 2 _____ _____	_____ _____ _____ _____
Transcendent	1 _____ _____ 2 _____ _____	_____ _____ _____ _____
Omniscient	1 _____ _____ 2 _____ _____	_____ _____ _____ _____
Benevolent	1 _____ _____ 2 _____ _____	_____ _____ _____ _____

B Now answer the following questions.

1. Give **one** reason why the 99 names of God can help Muslims to understand God.

_____

_____

_____

2. Give **one** way Muslims might use the 99 names of God.

_____

_____

Activity 3.12: The influence of God's nature on Christians today

 Christianity: pages 118–119

For each of the following attributes of God, explain what it might mean for a Christian in their lives today. One has been done for you as an example.

Attribute	What does this mean for Christians today?
Omnipotent	Knowing that God is all-powerful can inspire a feeling of awe and respect. It helps Christians to trust God because they know he has the power to do anything he wants. Also, because Christians believe God was powerful enough to create the universe, Christians will try to look after his creation.
Omniscient	
Personal	
Immanent	
Transcendent	
Benevolent	

Sources of religious belief and teaching

 Christianity: pages 118–119
Islam: pages 104–105

Some quotations about God from the Bible and the Qur'an are given below. For each quotation, decide which of the characteristics in the box below it best describes. Then in the right-hand column, explain how the quotation shows that this is a characteristic of God.

Omnipotent

Omniscient

Personal

Impersonal

Immanent

Transcendent

Quotation	Characteristic of God	How the quotation shows this
"The heavens declare the glory of God; the skies proclaim the work of his hands." *Psalm* 19:1		
"When there is a prophet among you, I, the LORD, reveal myself to them in visions, I speak to them in dreams." *Numbers* 12:6		
"He is God the One, God the eternal. He begot no one nor was He begotten. No one is comparable to Him." *Qur'an* 112		
"Travel throughout the earth and see how He brings life into being. God has power over all things." *Qur'an* 29:20		

Activity 3.13: Arguments for and against the existence of God

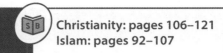

Christianity: pages 106–121
Islam: pages 92–107

Some arguments for and against the existence of God are given below. Decide if each one is more likely to be used to support theism or atheism. Then give a counter-argument to show how a theist might respond to an atheist argument, and vice versa. One has been done for you as an example.

Argument	Does it support theism or atheism?	How might a theist or atheist respond with a counter-argument?
Good people die from horrible diseases	Atheism	God has a plan for everyone and suffering is a natural part of life.
We have scientific evidence of evolution		
Everything in the universe has a cause		
People have had visions of Jesus or God		
People have recovered from serious illnesses after praying to God		
There is no proof of God		

Exam practice

Use your answers to Activity 3.13 to help you write a complete answer to this exam question.

'There is little evidence to prove the existence of God.'

Evaluate this statement.

In your answer you:

- should give reasoned arguments in support of this statement
- should give reasoned arguments to support a different point of view
- should refer to religious arguments
- may refer to non-religious arguments
- should reach a justified conclusion.

[12 marks]
[SPaG 3 marks]

TIP

If you have time, give yourself a minute or two to plan your answer. You are allowed to annotate the statement and/or write a plan in the space given. However, make sure you cross out anything that isn't for the examiner to mark as part of your answer.

Activity 3.14: The value of revelation

Christianity: pages 120–121
Islam: pages 106–107

Answer the following questions about the value of revelation.

1. Give **two** reasons why revelations are valuable to people.

_____

_____

_____

_____

2. Give **two** ways that we might determine whether a revelation is real or not.

_____

_____

_____

_____

3. Give **two** alternative explanations that atheists might put forward for revelations.

_____

_____

_____

_____

_____

Key terms

Christianity: pages 106–121
Islam: pages 92–107

Some key terms are very similar, so it is important to know what the difference is between them.
Carefully define each key term below to make sure you can distinguish between them.

Key term 1	Key term 2
Theist	Atheist
Omnipotent	Omniscient
Immanent	Transcendent
Revelation	Enlightenment

Key Terms Glossary

As you progress through the course, you can collect the meanings of useful terms in the glossary below. You can then use the completed glossaries to revise from.

To do well in the exam you will need to understand these terms and include them in your answers. Tick the shaded circles to record how confident you feel.

The First Cause argument _____

○ I recognise this term

◐ I understand what this term means

● I can use this term in a sentence

Atheist _____

General revelation _____

The Design argument _____

Humanist _____

Divine _____

Immanent _____

Enlightenment _____

Impersonal _____

Evil _____

Miracle _____

Nature _____

_____

_____

_____

_____

Special revelation _____

_____

_____

_____

_____

Omnipotent _____

_____

_____

_____

_____

Suffering _____

_____

_____

_____

_____

Omniscient _____

_____

_____

_____

_____

Theist _____

_____

_____

_____

_____

Personal _____

_____

_____

_____

_____

Transcendent _____

_____

_____

_____

_____

Revelation _____

_____

_____

_____

_____

Ultimate reality _____

_____

_____

_____

_____

Scripture _____

_____

_____

_____

_____

Vision _____

_____

_____

_____

_____

Activity 4.1: Peace, justice, forgiveness and reconciliation

Christianity: pages 124–125
Islam: pages 110–111

A Four definitions are given in the table below. Match each one up to the correct term.

Peace   Justice   Forgiveness   Reconciliation

Definition	Term
Creating equality and fairness in society	
Restoring relationships after they have broken down	
A feeling of happiness and calmness	
Pardoning someone when they have done something wrong	

B Creating a peaceful world is important to both Christians and Muslims. Explain how each concept below can help to create peace.

Concept	How can it help to create peace?
Justice	
Forgiveness	
Reconciliation	

Activity 4.2: Answering an exam question on justice

Christianity: page 125
Islam: page 111

Two students have written an answer to the following exam question:

Explain **two** similar religious beliefs about justice.

In your answer you must refer to one or more religious traditions.   **[4 marks]**

Read each of the answers below. Identify what each student has done well and what they could do to improve their work.

TIP

When reading each answer, think about the following:
- Is it factually correct and does it make sense?
- Has the student made good use of key terms?
- Has the student added detail and explanation to their points?
- Are the religious beliefs similar?

Student 1

In Isaiah it says that God will bring justice as the ultimate judge. Allah is just.

What they've done well	What they can do to improve their answer

Student 2

Some Christians believe that God will bring justice when we are judged on Judgement Day. We will be rewarded for our good actions by being with Him in heaven.

Some Muslims say that humans should bring about justice in the world by following the teachings in the Qur'an. For example, teachings about how to treat other people fairly and how to punish people who have done wrong.

What they've done well	What they can do to improve their answer

Activity 4.3: Violent protest and terrorism

 Christianity: pages 126–127
Islam: pages 112–113

Answer these questions about violent protest and terrorism.

1. Why was there rioting in London in 2011?

_____

_____

_____

2. How did religious leaders and groups in London respond to the rioting?

_____

_____

_____

3. How did Dr Martin Luther King Jr help to reduce inequality for black people in the US in the 1950s and 1960s?

_____

_____

_____

4. Given your understanding of Christianity, do you think that most Christians would support a violent protest demanding better rights for racial minorities in the UK? Explain your answer.

_____

_____

_____

_____

5. Give a definition of the word 'terrorism'.

_____

_____

_____

6. Why do Muslims condemn terrorism? Explain using a reference to scripture.

_____

_____

_____

_____

Activity 4.4: Reasons for war

 Christianity: pages 128–129
Islam: pages 114–115

The table below gives some examples of wars that have happened in the past.

Decide what you think was the reason for each of these wars. Was it greed, self-defence, retaliation or another reason?

Then consider if you think religious believers would find this reason to be justified or not and explain why.

Example	Reason(s)	Would religious believers think it was justified? Why?
During the Second World War the UK fought against Nazi invasion as they saw it as an evil threat to the whole of Europe.		
In 2001, the US government ordered military action against Afghanistan in response to the belief that they were involved in the 9/11 attacks in the US. The US government believed that Afghanistan was providing shelter for the leader of Al-Qaeda, Osama Bin Laden.		
In the Gulf War of 1990/1991, Iraq invaded Kuwait to take control of their oil fields and resources.		
In Muslim countries such as Iraq, Iran and Libya around the start of the twenty-first century, Muslim citizens chose to fight to overthrow what they felt were unjust leaders, wanting the opportunity to have a more democratic government.		

Exam practice

Now answer the following exam question.

Give **two** religious beliefs about the reasons for war.

[2 marks]

1 ~~One~~ One religion belief is that Christians believe that war is only allowed in self-defence.

2 Another religious belief is that Muslims believe ~~that~~ in Lesser Jihad, which is the struggle to defend ones country

Activity 4.5: Nuclear weapons and weapons of mass destruction

SB Christianity: pages 130–131
Islam: pages 116–117

A There are many arguments for and against possessing or using nuclear weapons and weapons of mass destruction. Decide if each of the arguments below is **for** or **against** their possession and use.

	For	Against
They act as a deterrent to other countries that may want to attack.	☐	☐
They have the potential to destroy the entire world.	☐	☐
They are very expensive to build and maintain.	☐	☐
In the past they have stopped wars (e.g. the Hiroshima atomic bomb).	☐	☐
If other countries have them then the only way to fight is with the same weapons.	☐	☐

TIP

When you are writing about nuclear weapons, remember there is a difference between possessing them and using them. Some people agree with possessing them but not with using them.

B Two arguments against the use of nuclear weapons are given below. For each of these arguments, explain what a religious response (either Christian or Muslim) might be.

Argument	Religious response
They kill large numbers of innocent civilians	
They destroy and contaminate landscapes that may never recover	

Activity 4.6: Just war conditions

 Christianity: pages 132–133

The main conditions of a just war in Christianity are given below. Some people claim that it is impossible to have a truly just war that fulfils all these conditions.

Choose **three** of the conditions and explain why it might be difficult to fulfil them.

The war must have a just cause	The war must be declared by the correct authority	The intention of the war has to be to defeat wrongdoing and promote good
Fighting must be a last resort	There must be a reasonable chance of success	The methods used to fight the war must be proportional; excessive force should not be used
The war must be fought by just means	Innocent people and civilians must not be targeted or harmed	Internationally agreed rules and conventions must be obeyed

Condition	Why it might be difficult to fulfil

Exam practice

Now answer the following exam question.

Which **one** of the following is not a condition for a just war? **[1 mark]**

A There must be a reasonable chance of success

B The war must have a just cause

C The war must be agreed by both sides

D The war must be declared by the correct authority

Activity 4.7: Religious attitudes towards a just war

 **Christianity: pages 132–133
Islam: pages 118–119**

Four conditions for a just war are given below. For each one, give a religious belief or teaching that might be used to support it from either Islam or Christianity.

Condition	Religious belief or teaching
The intention of the war has to be to defeat wrongdoing and promote good	
Innocent people and civilians must not be targeted or harmed	
Fighting must be a last resort	
The war must be declared by the correct authority	

Activity 4.8: Lesser jihad

 Islam: pages 118–119

Some of the conditions for lesser jihad are given in the table below. For each condition, decide which of the following quotations from the Qur'an could be used to support it. Write the relevant number in the right-hand column of the table.

1.

❝they give food to the poor, the orphan, and the captive, though they love it themselves.❞

Qur'an 76:8

2.

❝Fight in God's cause against those who fight you, but do not overstep the limits: God does not love those who overstep the limits.❞

Qur'an 2:190

3.

❝Those who have been attacked are permitted to take up arms because they have been wronged – God has the power to help them.❞

Qur'an 22:39

4.

❝though if a person is patient and forgives, this is one of the greatest things.❞

Qur'an 42:43

5.

❝If you [believers] have to respond to an attack, make your response proportionate, but it is best to stand fast.❞

Qur'an 16:126

6.

❝Why should you not fight in God's cause and for those oppressed men, women, and children who cry out, 'Lord, rescue us from this town whose people are oppressors!'❞

Qur'an 4:75

Condition	Supporting quotation
The war is a last resort – fighting must be the last option only when diplomacy and negotiation have failed	
The reason for the war is self-defence – the initial aggression should come from the other side	
The reason for the war is to protect innocent people who are being mistreated	
Prisoners should be treated in a civilised way	
Fighting should be without anger	
Wars should be fought with only the necessary amount of force	

Challenge activity 4.9: An evaluation of two wars

 Christianity: pages 132–133
Islam: pages 118–119

| World War One | World War Two | The Falklands War | The Gulf War | The Iraq War |

Choose **two** of the wars above to research. For each one, fill in the table below to show:

- what you think were the main reason(s) for the war

- which of the just war criteria you think the war did *not* fulfil, and why

- whether you think the war would have been approved by religious believers, and why.

TIP

You are not required to know about specific wars for your exam, but it is useful to consider whether wars in the real world can be 'just' or not, and if relevant you can use examples of wars in your answers to help develop your points or give evidence for a reason.

Name of the war	
Main reasons for the war	
Which of the just war criteria were NOT fulfilled? Why?	
Approved by religious believers? Why or why not?	

Name of the war	
Main reasons for the war	
Which of the just war criteria were NOT fulfilled? Why?	
Approved by religious believers? Why or why not?	

Activity 4.10: Holy war

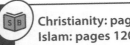 Christianity: pages 134–135
Islam: pages 120–121

A Decide if the following statements about holy war in Islam are true or false. If a statement is false, use the space in the table to correct it so it is true.

Statement	True/False	If false, what is the correct statement?
Muhammad fought in a holy war		
A holy war can be used to convert people to Islam		
A holy war should be fought for God		
A holy war must be declared by a political leader		
Any Muslim killed when fighting in a holy war will go to paradise		

B Now decide if the following statements about holy war in Christianity are true or false. As above, correct any false statements so they are true.

Statement	True/False	If false, what is the correct statement?
There are examples of holy war in the Old Testament		
A holy war can be started by any Christian in the name of God		
The purpose of a holy war is to expand the Kingdom of God		
Any Christian that dies during a holy war will be punished in the afterlife		
Christian teachings do not encourage using violence to defend the faith		

Sources of religious belief and teaching

(S)(B) Christianity: page 131

Read the quotations below and then answer the following questions.

A

"But if there is serious injury, you are to take life for life, eye for eye, tooth for tooth, hand for hand, foot for foot…"
Exodus 21:23–24

1. Why do some people think this quotation from the Old Testament justifies fighting in retaliation?

_____
_____
_____
_____

2. When this quotation was first written, did it support or oppose the use of excessive violence? Explain your answer.

_____
_____
_____
_____

B

"You have heard that it was said 'Eye for eye, and tooth for tooth'. But I tell you, do not resist an evil person. If anyone slaps you on the right cheek, turn to them the other cheek also."
Matthew 5:38–39

1. Jesus spoke the words above to his followers. What do you think he was telling his followers about the 'eye for eye' quotation?

_____
_____
_____
_____

2. Jesus gave many teachings about violence. Give another one of his teachings about violence and explain what it means.

_____
_____
_____
_____

TIP
Do you remember that one of Jesus' most famous teachings is about how to treat your neighbour? This teaching could be linked to violence.

Exam practice

Use your answers to the previous two activities to write an answer to this exam question.

Explain **two** religious beliefs about holy war.

Refer to sacred writings or another source of religious belief and teaching in your answer.　**[5 marks]**

_____
_____
_____
_____
_____
_____
_____
_____
_____
_____
_____
_____
_____

Activity 4.11: Charlie Hebdo　　　　　　　　　　Islam: page 121

Complete this fact file about the *Charlie Hebdo* terrorist attack in January 2015.

Where did the attack take place?	
Why did the attack happen?	
What did the two attackers do?	
How did most Muslims respond to the attack?	

TIP

Being able to give specific examples is useful in the 4-mark, 5-mark and 12-mark questions. You could use the *Charlie Hebdo* attack as an example when writing about terrorism.

Sources of religious belief and teaching

 Christianity: pages 136–137
Islam: pages 122–123

A Each quotation below has a box in the top left-hand corner.

- Tick this box if you think the quotation supports pacifism and peacemaking.

- Put a question mark in the box if you think the quotation is ambiguous (it could be used to either support or oppose pacifism and peacemaking).

- Put a cross in the box if you do not think the quotation supports pacifism and peacemaking.

> **"** Those who have been attacked are permitted to take up arms because they have been wronged – God has the power to help them. **"**
>
> *Qur'an 22:39*

> **"** But I tell you that anyone who is angry with a brother or sister will be subject to judgement. **"**
>
> *Matthew 5:22*

> **"** If you [believers] have to respond to an attack, make your response proportionate, but it is best to stand fast. **"**
>
> *Qur'an 16:126*

> **"** But if there is a serious injury, you are to take life for life, eye for eye, tooth for tooth…. **"**
>
> *Exodus 21:23–24*

> **"** Fight in God's cause against those who fight you, but do not overstep the limits: God does not love those who overstep the limits. **"**
>
> *Qur'an 2:190*

> **"** Blessed are the peacemakers, for they will be called children of God. **"**
>
> *Matthew 5:9*

> **"** … Jesus went up to Jerusalem. In the temple courts he found people selling cattle, sheep and doves, and others sitting at tables exchanging money. So he made a whip out of cords, and drove all from the temple courts, both sheep and cattle; he scattered the coins of the money-changers and overturned their tables. **"**
>
> *John 2:13–15*

> **"** …there is cause to act against those who oppress people and transgress in the land against all justice… though if a person is patient and forgives, this is one of the greatest things. **"**
>
> *Qur'an 42:42–43*

> **"** But if they [non-believers] incline towards peace, you [Prophet] must also incline towards it, and put your trust in God: He is the All Hearing, the All Knowing. **"**
>
> *Qur'an 8:61*

B Refer to some of the quotations above to explain either Muslim or Christian views towards pacifism and peacemaking.

_____

_____

_____

_____

TIP

Remember that there are often divergent views towards a topic within Christianity or Islam. Try to reflect this in your writing, for example by saying 'Some Christians believe…' or 'Most Catholics believe…' rather than 'All Christians believe…'

Activity 4.12: Religious organisations that promote peace

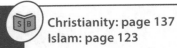

Christianity: page 137
Islam: page 123

Answer these questions about religious organisations that promote peace.

Christianity

1. What is the Anglican Pacifist Fellowship?

_____

_____

_____

2. What do they believe?

_____

_____

_____

3. What do they do?

_____

_____

_____

Islam

4. What is the Muslim Peace Fellowship?

_____

_____

_____

5. What do they believe?

_____

_____

_____

6. What do they do?

_____

_____

_____

Exam practice

Use your answers to the previous two activities to help you write a complete answer to this exam question.

'All religious believers should be pacifists.'

Evaluate this statement.

In your answer you:

- should give reasoned arguments in support of this statement
- should give reasoned arguments to support a different point of view
- should refer to religious arguments
- may refer to non-religious arguments
- should reach a justified conclusion.

[12 marks]
[SPaG 3 marks]

TIP

Make sure that your answer includes clear references to religion, linking to the statement. This can include beliefs, teachings and references to sources of wisdom and authority.

Activity 4.13: Religious organisations that help victims of war

Christianity: pages 138–139
Islam: pages 124–125

Choose one Christian and one Muslim religious organisation that works with victims of war. Complete the tables below with information about each of them.

Name of Christian organisation	
Three things the organisation does to support victims of war	1
	2
	3
A quotation from a source of religious belief and teaching that supports their aims	

Name of Muslim organisation	
Three things the organisation does to support victims of war	1
	2
	3
A quotation from a source of religious belief and teaching that supports their aims	

Exam practice

Now answer the following exam question.

Explain **two** similar religious beliefs about helping victims of war.   **[4 marks]**

_____

_____

_____

_____

_____

_____

_____

_____

_____

TIP

If a 4-mark question asks for similar beliefs it means stating two views that have the same attitude to the issue (although these views could be for different reasons).

Activity 4.14: Evaluating arguments about war and violence

 Christianity: pages 124–139
Islam: pages 110–125

Decide whether you think the following arguments about war and violence are strong or weak and explain why.

Argument	Is this a strong or weak argument? Why?
Jesus never fought in a war so Christians should not fight in wars today.	

TIP

You might consider an argument to be strong if it is supported by a core religious belief or teaching or it seems logical. You might consider an argument to be weak if it is just a personal opinion, there is no strong evidence to support it, it is illogical, or it only applies in some situations.

Jesus taught 'But I tell you, do not resist an evil person. If anyone slaps you on the right cheek, turn to them the other cheek also' (*Matthew* 5:39). This means Christians should not fight even in self-defence.	
The Qur'an says that 'Fighting has been ordained for you, though it is hard for you' (*Qur'an* 2:216). This means that Muslims cannot be pacifists.	
The concept of holy war means that Christians today should be allowed to use violence to defend their faith.	

Key terms	Christianity: pages 124–139 Islam: pages 110–125

Some key terms are very similar, so it is important to know what the difference is between them. Carefully define each key term below to make sure you can distinguish between them.

Key term 1	Key term 2
Forgiveness	Reconciliation
Violence	Terrorism
Just war	Holy war
Lesser jihad	Greater jihad
Pacifism	Peacemaking
Self-defence	Retaliation
Riot	Protest

Key Terms Glossary

As you progress through the course, you can collect the meanings of useful terms in the glossary below. You can then use the completed glossaries to revise from.

To do well in the exam you will need to understand these terms and include them in your answers. Tick the shaded

circles to record how confident you feel. Use the extra boxes at the end to record any other terms that you have found difficult, along with their definitions.

○ **I recognise this term**

◐ **I understand what this term means**

● **I can use this term in a sentence**

Forgiveness _____

Greed _____

Holy war _____

Just war _____

Justice _____

Nuclear deterrence _____

Nuclear weapons _____

Pacifism _____

Peace _____

Peacemaking _____

Reconciliation _____

Retaliation

Weapons of mass destruction

Self-defence

Terrorism

Victims of war

Violence

Violent protest

Chapter 5: **Theme E: Religion, crime and punishment**

Activity 5.1: Muslim attitudes towards intentions and actions Islam: page 129

Read the Hadith below explaining how important intentions and actions are to Muslims. Then answer the questions below.

> " Allah has recorded good and evil deeds and he made them clear. Whoever intends to perform a good deed but does not do it, then Allah will record it as a complete good deed. If he intends to do it and does so, then Allah Almighty will record it as ten good deeds, up to seven hundred times as much or even more. If he intends to do an evil deed and does not do it, then Allah will record for him one complete good deed. If he does it, then Allah will record for him a single evil deed. "

1. List **three** things that Muslims might consider to be 'good deeds'.

_____

_____

_____

2. List **three** things that Muslims might consider to be 'bad deeds'.

_____

_____

_____

3. Why do you think that having a bad intention but not carrying it out is classed as a 'good deed'?

_____

_____

_____

_____

4. According to Islam, why do some people do 'evil' deeds?

_____

_____

_____

5. How does the writing down of deeds link to Muslim beliefs about life after death?

_____

_____

_____

TIP

See pages 18–19 in the Islam student book to remind yourself about what happens on the Day of Judgement.

89

Activity 5.2: Christian attitudes towards intentions and actions

 Christianity: page 143

One criteria a Christian might use to decide whether an action is 'good' or 'evil' is whether it is legal or illegal in the country in which they live.

1. Give **three** other criteria a Christian might use to decide whether an action is 'good' or 'evil'.

1 _____

2 _____

3 _____

2. According to Christianity, why do some people do 'evil' things?

_____

_____

_____

3. Christians believe that God knows what their intentions are even if they do not act on them or share them with anyone else. Explain why Christians believe that God knows people's intentions.

_____

_____

_____

_____

_____

Exam practice

Use your answers to the previous two activities to write an answer to this exam question.

Explain **two** similar religious beliefs about good and evil intentions and actions.

In your answer you must refer to one or more religious traditions.

[4 marks]

_____

_____

_____

_____

_____

_____

_____

_____

_____

_____

Activity 5.3: Reasons for crime

SB **Christianity: pages 144–145**
Islam: pages 130–131

Some of the reasons why people commit crime include:

Opposition to an unjust law

Hate

Greed

Why people commit crime

Addiction

Mental illness

Poverty

Upbringing

TIP

Your answers could include:
- whether there are any religious teachings that might guide Christians or Muslims as to what to believe
- how Christians or Muslims might help to solve these reasons for crime.

Choose **three** of these reasons and explain religious responses to them.

Reason:	
Christian response	
Muslim response	

Reason:	
Christian response	
Muslim response	

Reason:	
Christian response	
Muslim response	

Activity 5.4: Categories of crime in Shari'ah law

Islam: page 133

A Shari'ah law classifies crimes into four different types. Sort the crimes below by adding them into the correct box.

- speeding
- adultery
- parking fine
- murder

- theft
- bodily harm
- graffiti
- antisocial behaviour

Unforgivable crimes

_____

_____

Forgivable crimes

_____

_____

Community crimes

_____

_____

Crimes against the state law

_____

_____

B Now answer the following questions.

1. How do you think Muslims might decide if a crime is 'forgivable' or 'unforgivable'?

_____

_____

_____

_____

2. Drinking alcohol is forbidden in Islam and classed as an unforgivable crime. Why might this be the case?

_____

_____

_____

3. Most surahs in the Qur'an begin with 'In the Name of Allah the most merciful'. What might this tell us about forgiveness in Islam?

_____

_____

_____

Activity 5.5: Christian attitudes to different types of crime

SB **Christianity: pages 146–147**

For each type of crime below, explain Christian views towards it. Then give a relevant quotation from a source of religious belief and teaching and explain how it supports these views.

TIP When you use a quotation to support a view, it is useful to explain how it is relevant. This helps link it to the point you are making.

Hate crime	
Christian attitudes towards hate crimes:	
Quotation:	
Why this quotation is relevant:	

Theft	
Christian attitudes towards theft:	
Quotation:	
Why this quotation is relevant:	

Murder	
Christian attitudes towards murder:	
Quotation:	
Why this quotation is relevant:	

Exam practice

Use your answers to the previous two activities to write an answer to this exam question.

Explain **two** religious beliefs about theft.

Refer to sacred writings or another source of religious belief and teaching in your answer.

[5 marks]

_____

_____

_____

_____

_____

_____

_____

_____

_____

_____

_____

_____

_____

_____

Activity 5.6: The purposes of different punishments

SB Christianity: pages 148–149
Islam: pages 136–137

Tick the relevant boxes to show whether you think the punishments below are examples of retribution, deterrence or reformation. (You may want to tick more than one box for each punishment if you think it covers more than one aim.)

	Retribution	Deterrence	Reformation
Prison	☐	☐	☐
A driving ban	☐	☐	☐
Counselling	☐	☐	☐
The death penalty	☐	☐	☐
Meeting the victim	☐	☐	☐
Community service	☐	☐	☐
Corporal punishment	☐	☐	☐

Activity 5.7: Three aims of punishment

Christianity: pages 148–149
Islam: pages 136–137

Answer these questions on the three aims of punishment in Christianity and Islam.

1. Does the Bible quotation 'eye for eye, tooth for tooth' support retribution or reformation? Explain your answer.

_____

_____

_____

_____

2. Which aim of punishment do most Christians prefer?

_____

3. Why do you think most Christians prefer this aim?

_____

_____

_____

4. Why do some Muslims prefer that compensation is given instead of the death penalty for a crime such as murder?

_____

_____

_____

_____

5. Name **two** crimes under Shari'ah law that aren't crimes in the UK.

_____

_____

6. Give **two** reasons why Shari'ah punishments deter others from committing crimes.

_____

_____

_____

_____

Exam practice

Now answer the following exam question.

Which **one** of the following has the aim of putting people off committing crimes?   **[1 mark]**

A Deterrence

B Retaliation

C Retribution

D Reformation

Activity 5.8: Suffering in Islam

 Islam: pages 134–135

Explain how each of these key concepts link to Muslim beliefs about suffering.

Concept	How does it link to Muslim beliefs about suffering?
Life as a test	
Iblis	
Free will	
Ummah	
Adam and Hawwa (Eve)	

Activity 5.9: Suffering in Christianity

 Christianity: pages 150–151

The Bible tells Christians about what suffering is and how they should respond to it. Read these Bible passages and explain what each one tells Christians about suffering.

Quotation	How it links to Christian beliefs about suffering
"we also glory in our sufferings, because we know that suffering produces perseverance; perseverance, character; and character, hope." *Romans 5:3–4*	
"And wherever he went – into villages, towns or countryside – they placed those who were ill in the market-places. They begged him to let them touch even the edge of his cloak, and all who touched it were healed." *Mark 6:56*	
"In fact, everyone who wants to live a godly life in Christ Jesus will be persecuted." *2 Timothy 3:12*	
"Carry each other's burdens, and in this way you will fulfil the law of Christ." *Galatians 6:2*	
"But I tell you, love your enemies and pray for those who persecute you." *Matthew 5:44*	

Activity 5.10: The treatment of criminals

Christianity: pages 152–153
Islam: pages 138–139

A Decide if the statements below about the treatment of criminals in Islam are true or false. If a statement is false, use the space in the table to correct it so it is true.

Statement	True/False	If false, what is the correct statement?
Under Shari'ah law, prisons should mainly be used to hold criminals awaiting trial or punishment		
Corporal punishment is against Shari'ah law		
Public caning or flogging is illegal in all Muslim countries		
Shari'ah law is mainly about reformation		
Some Muslims believe that Shari'ah punishments are too harsh		

B Now decide if the following statements about the treatment of criminals in Christianity are true or false. As above, correct any false statements so they are true.

Statement	True/False	If false, what is the correct statement?
Most Christians would agree with using prisons to reform criminals		
Christians disagree with the use of discipline and punishment		
Most Christians view corporal punishment as against human rights		
Jesus said we should punish people that do wrong		
Most Christians would say corporal punishment is better than community service		

Activity 5.11: Religious attitudes to forgiveness

Christianity: pages 154–155
Islam: pages 140–141

A Using the terms below, write an entire paragraph to explain Christian attitudes towards forgiveness.

| Jesus | forgiveness | crucifixion | God | Lord's Prayer | punishment | justice |

_____

_____

_____

_____

_____

_____

_____

_____

_____

_____

_____

_____

_____

_____

B Now use the terms below to write an entire paragraph about Muslim attitudes towards forgiveness.

| God | merciful | forgiveness | humans | ask | Shari'ah law | death penalty |

_____

_____

_____

_____

_____

_____

_____

_____

_____

_____

_____

_____

_____

Sources of religious belief and teaching

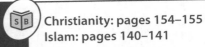

Christianity: pages 154–155
Islam: pages 140–141

The sentences below could be used to answer an exam question on forgiveness. For each sentence, suggest a relevant source of religious belief or teaching that could be used to develop it. One example has been done for you.

1. Christians believe that Jesus told them to forgive. This shows that forgiveness is very important.

   In the Bible he said we should forgive 'seventy-seven times'.

   _____

2. Muslims believe that Allah forgives us for our sins. This doesn't mean we can do whatever we want at any time but when we do something wrong, we can ask him for forgiveness.

   _____

   _____

3. Christians believe that Jesus forgave other people even when they had done things wrong. This means that we should also forgive other people.

   _____

   _____

4. Muslims believe that if you want to be forgiven by Allah then you must forgive other people. This means that Muslims should show mercy to others.

   _____

   _____

5. Christians believe that we should forgive other people when they do something wrong to us. We would want God to forgive us so we should forgive them.

   _____

   _____

Exam practice

Now answer the following exam question.

Give **two** religious beliefs about forgiveness.   **[2 marks]**

1 _____

   _____

2 _____

   _____

Key terms

 Christianity: pages 142–157
Islam: pages 128–143

Some key terms are very similar, so it is important to know what the difference is between them. Carefully define each key term below to make sure you can distinguish between them.

TIP The 1-mark questions in the exam will include multiple-choice options that might be very similar. This is one reason why it is useful to be able to distinguish between similar key terms.

Key term 1	Key term 2
Crime	Hate crime
Punishment	Forgiveness
Intention	Action
Retribution	Reformation
Corporal punishment	Capital punishment

Activity 5.12: Arguments for and against the death penalty

 Christianity: pages 156–157
Islam: pages 142–143

Read these arguments for and against the death penalty. Write 'for' or 'against' underneath each one depending on whether you think it could be used to support or oppose the death penalty. Then answer the questions below.

TIP An argument might be considered strong if it is supported by a core religious belief or teaching, it seems logical, or many people agree with it. An argument might be considered weak if it is just a personal opinion, it seems illogical, there is little evidence to support it or the evidence that is used is flawed in some way.

God gives life and only God should take life (the sanctity of life)	Innocent people are sometimes mistakenly killed	It is a deterrent for society
It is the best thing to do for the greatest number of people (the principle of utility)	It is against human rights	It protects society by getting rid of people that are dangerous
It follows the teaching 'an eye for an eye'	It has been used for thousands of years	Rehabilitation and reform are more loving

1. Choose an argument that you think is the weakest, and explain why you think it is a weak argument.

_____

_____

_____

_____

_____

_____

2. Choose an argument that you think is the strongest, and explain why you think it is a strong argument.

_____

_____

_____

_____

_____

_____

_____

Sources of religious belief and teaching

 Christianity: pages 156–157

Here are some quotations that could influence Christian views on the death penalty. Explain what each quotation suggests about whether the death penalty should be used in modern society, and why. If the quotation suggests the death penalty should not be used, does it suggest an alternative course of action instead?

Quotation	What does it suggest about the use of the death penalty? Why?
" Whoever sheds human blood, by humans shall their blood be shed. **"** *Genesis* 9:6	
" Life for life, eye for eye, tooth for tooth. **"** *Exodus* 21:23–24	
" I take no pleasure in the death of the wicked, but rather that they turn away from their ways and live. **"** *Ezekiel* 33:11	
" You shall not murder. **"** *Exodus* 20:13	
" Every life is sacred, every human person is endowed with an inalienable dignity, and society can only benefit from the rehabilitation of those convicted of crimes. **"** *Pope Francis*	

Activity 5.13: Use of the death penalty in Islam

 Islam: pages 142–143

Complete the boxes below to summarise the use of the death penalty in Islam.

Three crimes that the death penalty is used for in Shari'ah law	Three methods used to carry out the death penalty under Shari'ah law
• _____ _____ • _____ _____ • _____ _____	• _____ _____ • _____ _____ • _____ _____
Three reasons why the death penalty might not be used for a serious crime	**Three reasons why some Muslims oppose the use of the death penalty**
• _____ _____ _____ _____ • _____ _____ _____ _____ • _____ _____ _____ _____	• _____ _____ _____ _____ • _____ _____ _____ _____ • _____ _____ _____ _____

Exam practice

Use your answers to the previous two activities to help you write an answer to this exam question.

'All murderers should be executed with the death penalty.'

Evaluate this statement.

In your answer you:

- should give reasoned arguments in support of this statement
- should give reasoned arguments to support a different point of view
- should refer to religious arguments
- may refer to non-religious arguments
- should reach a justified conclusion.

[12 marks]
[SPaG 3 marks]

TIP

Your answer should have logical chains of reasoning. One way to achieve this is to think of it like a debate where different views are presented and evaluated, by taking turns in an organised way.

_____

_____

_____

_____

_____

_____

_____

_____

_____

_____

_____

_____

_____

_____

_____

_____

_____

_____

_____

_____

_____

Challenge activity 5.14: Sources of wisdom and authority

 Christianity: pages 142–157
Islam: pages 128–143

Each of the quotations below could be used to support punishment. For each one, give a religious counter-argument that explains why this behaviour is wrong, and what behaviour would be better instead. If possible, include a source of religious belief and teaching to support your argument.

> TIP Revising arguments and counter-arguments on key topics is a good way to prepare for a 12-mark question.

Argument	Counter-argument
Christianity	
"Whoever spares the rod hates their children." *Proverbs* 13:24	
"Whoever sheds human blood, by humans shall their blood be shed." *Genesis* 9:6	
Islam	
"Cut off the hands of thieves, whether they are man or woman, in return for what they have done – a deterrent from God." *Qur'an* 5:38	
"Do not take life, which God has made sacred, except by right." *Qur'an* 17:33	

Key Terms Glossary

As you progress through the course, you can collect the meanings of useful terms in the glossary below. You can then use the completed glossaries to revise from.

To do well in the exam you will need to understand these terms and include them in your answers. Tick the shaded circles to record how confident you feel. Use the extra boxes at the end to record any other terms that you have found difficult, along with their definitions.

○ **I recognise this term**

◐ **I understand what this term means**

● **I can use this term in a sentence**

Actions

Community service

Corporal punishment

Crime

Death penalty

Deterrence

Evil

Forgiveness

Good

Hate crime

Intentions

Law _____

_____

_____

_____

_____

Retribution _____

_____

_____

_____

Murder _____

_____

_____

_____

_____

Sanctity of life _____

_____

_____

_____

_____

Principle of utility _____

_____

_____

_____

_____

Suffering _____

_____

_____

_____

_____

Prison _____

_____

_____

_____

_____

Theft _____

_____

_____

_____

_____

Punishment _____

_____

_____

_____

_____

_____

_____

_____

_____

Reformation _____

_____

_____

_____

_____

_____

_____

_____

Chapter 6: Theme F: Religion, human rights and social justice

A Answer the following questions about social justice in Islam.

1. Explain why social justice and equality are important in Islam. Refer to both God and Muhammad in your answer.

2. Explain how paying Zakah helps to create social justice.

3. Give **one** more way that Muslims can help to promote social justice in the world today.

B Now answer the following questions.

1. Write a sentence explaining how human rights and social justice are linked.

2. Give **two** examples of things that Jesus said or did which teach Christians that they should promote social justice.

3. Give **one** way a Christian can help promote social justice in the world today.

Sources of religious belief and teaching

Christianity: pages 164–165
Islam: pages 150–151

Explain what each of the following quotations might mean for religious believers in regards to religious freedom. One has been done for you as an example.

Quotation	Meaning
Christianity	
❝Be completely humble and gentle; be patient, bearing with one another in love.❞ *Ephesians* 4:2	*Christians should show love and patience towards other people, regardless of their religion or beliefs.*
❝If it is possible, as far as it depends on you, live at peace with everyone.❞ *Romans* 12:18	
❝I urge you, brothers and sisters, to watch out for those who cause divisions and put obstacles in your way that are contrary to the teaching you have learned. Keep away from them.❞ *Romans* 16:17	
Islam	
❝Now the truth has come from your Lord: let those who wish to believe in it do so, and let those who wish to reject it do so.❞ *Qur'an* 18:29	
❝Do not try to justify yourselves; you have gone from belief to disbelief. We [Allah] may forgive some of you, but We [Allah] will punish others: they are evildoers.❞ *Qur'an* 9:66	
❝As for those who believe, then reject the faith, then believe again, then reject the faith again and become increasingly defiant, God will not forgive them, nor will He guide them on any path.❞ *Qur'an* 4:137	

Activity 6.2: Freedom of religious expression

Christianity: pages 164–165
Islam: pages 150–151

Answer these questions about freedom of religious expression.

1. What is the meaning of the phrase 'freedom of religious expression'?

_____

_____

_____

_____

2. One way that a Christian might express their religious beliefs is by wearing a cross around their neck. Give **three** other ways that a Christian or Muslim might express their religious beliefs in the UK today.

   1 _____

   _____

   2 _____

   _____

   3 _____

   _____

3. Give **two** ways that the government in the UK can help to protect freedom of religion and religious expression.

   _____

   _____

   _____

   _____

   _____

   _____

Exam practice

Now answer the following exam question.

Give **two** religious beliefs about freedom of religion.   **[2 marks]**

1 _____

_____

2 _____

_____

Activity 6.3: The status of women and homosexuals within the Church

Christianity: pages 162–163

A Some quotations, teachings and facts related to women and sexuality are given below. Decide whether each one could be used to:

1 support having female leaders in the Church (e.g. female priests and bishops)

2 oppose having female leaders in the Church

3 support same-sex marriage

4 oppose same-sex marriage

Add one or two numbers to each box depending on which of the point(s) above you think it relates to. One has been done for you as an example.

2

"Women should remain silent in the churches … for it is disgraceful for a woman to speak in the church."
1 Corinthians 14:34–35

"That is why a man leaves his father and mother and is united to his wife, and they become one flesh."
Genesis 2:24

Bible texts need to be interpreted in the context of modern society.

"Let everyone be subject to the governing authorities, for there is no authority except that which God has established."
Romans 13:1

"Love your neighbour as yourself."
Mark 12:31

Jesus chose men to be his disciples.

"So God created mankind in his own image, in the image of God he created them; male and female he created them."
Genesis 1:27

In Britain in 1993 the Church of England allowed women to be ordained as priests.

"Be fruitful and increase in number; fill the earth and subdue it."
Genesis 1:28

B Using some of the arguments on page 113, write a full paragraph to explain:

- contrasting Christian views on the status and treatment of women in Christianity
  or
- contrasting Christian views on the status and treatment of homosexuals in Christianity.

You can use one or more of the connectives given below, or you could use your own phrases to link the contrasting views.

Although	But	On the other hand	However
Whereas	In contrast	Alternatively	

_____

_____

_____

_____

_____

_____

_____

_____

TIP

Using connectives to link your sentences together can help you to write paragraphs that flow logically from one point to the next.

Activity 6.4: The roles of women in Islam

Islam: pages 154–155

Answer these questions about the roles of women in Islam.

1. Men and women are considered to be equal in Islam but they traditionally have different roles. Give **two** roles typically carried out by women in Islam and **two** roles typically carried out by men.

Roles carried out by women	Roles carried out by men
1 _____	1 _____
2 _____	2 _____

2. Why might some Muslims have different views on these roles and who should carry them out?

_____

_____

_____

_____

Exam practice

Now answer the following exam question.

Explain **two** religious beliefs about the roles of women in religion.

Refer to sacred writings or another source of religious belief and teaching in your answer.   **[5 marks]**

_____

_____

_____

_____

_____

_____

_____

_____

_____

_____

_____

_____

_____

Activity 6.5: Prejudice and discrimination

SB   **Christianity: pages 162–163**
     Islam: pages 152–153

Explain how each of the following helps to teach religious believers that prejudice and discrimination are wrong.

Muhammad's final sermon (Islam)	The clothing worn on Hajj (Islam)

Paul's letter to the Galatians (Christianity)	Agape love (Christianity)

Sources of wisdom and authority

 Christianity: pages 166–167
Islam: pages 152–153

A Choose **one** of the quotations below and explain how it could be used to support Christian opposition to racism.

1.
"There is neither Jew nor Gentile, neither slave nor free, nor is there male and female, for you are all one in Christ Jesus."
Galatians 3:28

2.
"I now realise how true it is that God does not show favouritism but accepts from every nation the one who fears him and does what is right."
Acts 10:34–35

3.
"Love your neighbour as yourself."
Matthew 22:39

_____

_____

_____

_____

_____

_____

B Choose **one** of the quotations below and explain how it could be used to support Muslim opposition to racism.

1.
"We are all equal as the teeth of a comb."
Hadith

2.
"No Arab is superior to a non-Arab, no coloured person to a white person, nor a white person to a coloured person except by piety."
Hadith

3.
"We [Allah] created you from a single man and a single woman, and made you into races and tribes so that you should get to know one another."
Qur'an 49:13

_____

_____

_____

_____

_____

_____

Activity 6.6: Positive discrimination

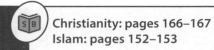

Christianity: pages 166–167
Islam: pages 152–153

Answer these questions about positive discrimination.

1. What do you think is the meaning of 'positive discrimination'?

_____

_____

_____

_____

2. Give **one** example of positive discrimination that might happen in the UK today.

_____

_____

_____

_____

3. Give **one** reason why a Christian or Muslim might agree with positive discrimination.

_____

_____

_____

_____

4. Give **one** reason why a Christian or Muslim might disagree with positive discrimination.

_____

_____

_____

_____

Exam practice

Now answer the following exam question.

Which one of the following means treating someone badly as a result of having an unfair opinion about them?   **[1 mark]**

A Prejudice

B Bias

C Discrimination

D Positive discrimination

Activity 6.7: Religious attitudes towards wealth

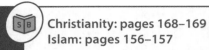

Christianity: pages 168–169
Islam: pages 156–157

A Decide if the statements below about Muslim attitudes towards wealth are true or false. If a statement is false, use the space in the table to correct it so it is true.

Statement	True/False	If false, what is the correct statement?
Muslims believe that wealth and riches are a blessing from God		
Muslims should hoard their money		
Muslims can obtain their wealth in any way they want		
Muslims believe God is testing them on how they use their wealth		
Zakah should only be used to help people go on Hajj		

B Now decide if the following statements about Christian attitudes towards wealth are true or false. As above, correct any false statements so they are true.

Statement	True/False	If false, what is the correct statement?
In the Old Testament God promised wealth to those who converted others to Christianity		
Using wealth to help other people is following Jesus		
The Parable of the Rich Man and Lazarus tells Christians to give all their money away		
In the Parable of the Sheep and the Goats, the reward for helping other people is money		
It shows agape to share wealth		

Activity 6.8: The uses and value of wealth

Christianity: pages 168–169
Islam: pages 156–157

Four different scenarios are given below. For two of these scenarios explain how you think Christians might respond, and for the other two scenarios explain how you think Muslims might respond. Would they approve of the person's decisions? Why or why not?

> I went into a career in banking because I wanted to become wealthy. I've worked hard to earn the money I've made.

_____

_____

_____

> I think that money is evil and the cause of many problems in the world. I try to rely on it as little as possible.

_____

_____

_____

> I make sure my family can live comfortably and we enjoy going on holiday occasionally. I save some money for the future and donate the rest to charity.

_____

_____

_____

> I applied for a loan for £1000 and I have to pay it back with 250% interest, which means I have to pay the loan company £3500 in total.

_____

_____

_____

Exam practice

Use your answers to the previous two activities to answer this exam question.

Explain **two** contrasting religious beliefs about the uses of wealth.   **[4 marks]**

_____

_____

_____

_____

_____

_____

_____

_____

_____

_____

_____

Activity 6.9: Poverty and its causes

 Christianity: pages 170–171
Islam: pages 158–159

A What do you think are some of the major causes of poverty and the most effective ways of combatting these causes? Complete the table below by giving three more causes and suggesting two actions that could be taken to help solve each of them.

Cause	What are the most effective ways of combatting this cause?
• Low wages	• Increase the minimum wage • Educate workers so they can find more skilled (and better paid) work
•	• •
•	• •
•	• •

B Which religious beliefs and teachings might tell Christians and Muslims how they can best help those living in poverty? Use the table below to list any relevant beliefs and teachings.

Christian beliefs and teachings about how to help those living in poverty	Muslim beliefs and teachings about how to help those living in poverty

Activity 6.10: Exploitation of the poor

Christianity: pages 172–173
Islam: pages 158–159

For each of the following issues, write down two short points that explain Christian and Muslim views towards the issue.

TIP You could explain *what* Christians and Muslims think about these issues and *why* they think this. Refer to sources of religious belief and teaching if possible.

Issue	Christian responses	Muslim responses
Fair pay	• _____ _____ • _____ _____	• _____ _____ • _____ _____
Interest on loans	• _____ _____ • _____ _____	• _____ _____ • _____ _____
People trafficking	• _____ _____ • _____	• _____ _____ • _____

Activity 6.11: Religious organisations that help the poor

Christianity: pages 174–175
Islam: pages 160–161

Choose one Christian and one Muslim religious organisation that works with people in poverty. Complete the tables below with information about them.

Name of Christian organisation	
Three things it does to support those in poverty	1
	2
	3
A quotation from a source of religious belief and teaching that would support its aims	

Name of Muslim organisation	
Three things it does to support those in poverty	1
	2
	3
A quotation from a source of religious belief and teaching that would support its aims	

Challenge activity 6.12: How best to help the poor

 Christianity: pages 174–175
Islam: pages 160–161

Answer the questions below on helping the poor.

1. Give **one** advantage and **one** disadvantage of short-term aid and long-term aid.

	Short-term (emergency) aid	**Long-term aid**
Advantage		
Disadvantage		

2. Charities rarely give money directly to the poor. Why do you think this is?

_____

_____

_____

_____

3. What criteria might affect how much responsibility a poor person should take for getting out of poverty themselves?

_____

_____

_____

_____

_____

> **TIP**
>
> One example might be whether there are suitable jobs available in the local area. What other factors might determine whether a poor person is able to take responsibility for getting out of poverty themselves, or whether they need more help from other people to do so?

4. Give **one** Christian or Muslim source of religious belief and authority that suggests the poor should take responsibility for getting out of poverty themselves.

_____

_____

5. How far do you think most Christians or Muslims would agree with this teaching?

_____

_____

_____

_____

Exam practice

Use your answers to the previous two activities to help you write a complete answer to this exam question.

'All religious believers should give 10% of their earnings to charity.'

Evaluate this statement.

In your answer you:

- should give reasoned arguments in support of this statement
- should give reasoned arguments to support a different point of view
- should refer to religious arguments
- may refer to non-religious arguments
- should reach a justified conclusion.

[12 marks]
[SPaG 3 marks]

TIP

The examiner will be looking for use of evidence and information in your answer. You can do this by including:
- Relevant keywords
- Quotations from sources of wisdom and authority
- Examples or case studies
- Evidence, possibly statistics
- Beliefs and teachings.

Key terms

Christianity: pages 160–175
Islam: pages 146–161

Some key terms are very similar, so it is important to know what the difference is between them.
Carefully define each key term below to make sure you can distinguish between them.

Key term 1	Key term 2
Social justice	Human rights
Prejudice	Discrimination
Freedom of religion	Freedom of religious expression
Exploitation	Poverty
Emergency aid	Long-term aid
Zakah	Khums

Key Terms Glossary

As you progress through the course, you can collect the meanings of useful terms in the glossary below. You can then use the completed glossaries to revise from.

To do well in the exam you will need to understand these terms and include them in your answers. Tick the shaded circles to record how confident you feel. Use the extra boxes at the end to record any other terms that you have found difficult, along with their definitions.

○ **I recognise this term**

◐ **I understand what this term means**

● **I can use this term in a sentence**

Exploitation

Charity

Fair pay

Discrimination

Freedom of religion and belief

Emergency aid

Freedom of religious expression

Equality

Human rights

Excessive interest on loans

Long-term aid

People-trafficking

Social justice

Positive discrimination

Wealth

Poverty

Prejudice

Racial discrimination

Racial prejudice

Test the 1-mark question

Example

1 Which **one** of the following means controlling how many children a couple has and when they have them? **[1 mark]**

A Contraception

B Procreation

C Family planning

D Nuclear family

C Family planning ✓ *(1)*

WHAT WILL THE QUESTION LOOK LIKE?

The 1-mark question will always be a **multiple-choice question** with four answers to choose from. Only one answer is correct. The question will usually start with the words **'Which one of the following…'**.

HOW IS IT MARKED?

You will receive 1 mark for a correct response.

> **! REMEMBER…**
>
> Read the question and the answers carefully before making your choice. Even if you are not sure of the right answer, make a guess – you may get it right anyway. It is time efficient and less likely to introduce any errors to just write A, B, C or D.

Activity

Theme A Which **one** of the following means being 'sexually attracted to members of the opposite sex'? **[1 mark]**

A Heterosexual

B Homosexual

C Bisexual

D Asexual

_____

Theme B Which **one** of the following describes looking after the Earth on behalf of God? **[1 mark]**

A Awe

B Dominion

C Stewardship

D Dependent arising

_____

Theme C Which **one** of the following is **not** an example of a special revelation? [1 mark]

A Miracle

B Vision

C Prophecy

D Pilgrimage

_____

Theme D Which **one** of the following is **not** a condition of a just war? [1 mark]

A Must be between two countries only

B Must be declared by a proper legal authority

C Must be a last resort

D Must have a reasonable chance of success

_____

Theme E Which **one** of the following is also known as capital punishment? [1 mark]

A The death penalty

B Prison

C Amputation of the hand

D Community service

_____

Theme F Which **one** of the following is **not** an example of discrimination? [1 mark]

A Paying men higher wages than women for the same job

B Thinking that all older people are inferior to younger people

C Asking for workers who are aged between 18 and 25 in a job advert

D Not allowing someone who is religious to attend an event

_____

Test the 2-mark question

Example

1 Give **two** religious beliefs about the role of parents.

Muslims believe it is the role of the mother to teach the children about Islam. ✓ *(1)*

Christians believe they should bring their children up to follow God's laws. ✓ *(1)*

! REMEMBER…

You need to give **two pieces of information** in your answer. Use the numbered lines to make sure you write two separate points. Don't just repeated yourself - make sure each point says something new.

Keep your answers short. You only need to provide two facts or short ideas; **you don't need to explain them or express any opinions**.

Activity

Theme A Give **two** religious reasons why some people are against divorce. **[2 marks]**

The sample answer below would get 1 mark because only one answer is correct. Cross out the wrong answer, then write another correct answer to earn a second mark.

In Islam, divorce is wrong.

In the Christian wedding vows it says 'till death do us part'.

_____

Theme B Give **two** types of euthanasia. **[2 marks]**

1 _____

_____

2 _____

_____

Theme C Give **two** ways that religious believers can experience general revelation. **[2 marks]**

1 _____

_____

2 _____

_____

Theme D Give **two** ways a present day religious organisation helps victims of war. [2 marks]

1 _____

_____

2 _____

_____

TIP

Try not to spend too much time on these questions. Ideally you should spend a maximum of 2 minutes on a 2-mark question.

Theme E Give **two** reasons for crime. [2 marks]

1 _____

_____

2 _____

_____

Theme F Give **two** religious beliefs about wealth. [2 marks]

1 _____

_____

2 _____

_____

Test the 4-mark question

Example

WHAT WILL THE QUESTION LOOK LIKE?

The 4-mark question will always start with the words **'Explain two…'**. It will ask you to give either **similar** or **contrasting** (different) religious beliefs. It may ask you to refer to the 'main religious tradition of Great Britain' (Christianity) in your answer, and for Theme C only (the existence of God and revelation) it may ask you to refer to Christianity and 'non-religious beliefs'.

1 Explain **two** contrasting religious beliefs about violent protest.

　　In your answer you must refer to one or more religious traditions. **[4 marks]**

Some Christians think that violent protest is acceptable in some circumstances when an important point needs to be made. ✓ **(1)** *They might follow the example of Jesus, who used violent protest when he turned over the tables of those trading in the temple.* ✓ **(1)**

Other Christians would disagree and say that peaceful protest is more effective. ✓ **(1)** *This is because it upholds the teaching to 'love your enemies' and can be seen successfully in the example of Martin Luther King Jr.* ✓ **(1)**

HOW IS IT MARKED?

This answer would gain 4 marks because it makes two different points, and both points are clearly developed. The two points also contrast with each other (they give different views on the issue).

! REMEMBER…

Try to show the examiner clearly where each belief begins. For example, you could start your answer with 'Some Christians believe…' and then move on to your second point by saying 'Other Christians believe…' or 'Some Muslims believe…'.

Try to **add detail** to each belief by giving an example or adding more explanation or a quotation. Adding detail to your points in this way will earn you more marks.

Activity

Theme A Explain **two** similar religious beliefs about abortion.

　　In your answer you must refer to one or more religious traditions. **[4 marks]**

The sample answer below would get 4 marks because there are two points, and each point has been developed. Add a tick next to each point. Then underline where each point has been developed.

Some Christians are against abortion as they consider the foetus to be alive and so it is classed as murder. The Bible is clear that murder is wrong when it says in the Ten Commandments 'do not kill'.

Some Muslims also believe that a foetus has a soul from conception and that it is considered to be alive, so abortion is wrong. To abort the foetus would be killing and the Qur'an says 'do not kill your children for fear of want'.

TIP

These beliefs are similar because they both disagree with abortion. It doesn't matter that different holy texts are used to support each belief – it is enough that the beliefs themselves are similar.

Theme B Explain **two** similar beliefs on animal experimentation.

　　In your answer you should refer to the main religious tradition of Great Britain and one or more other religious traditions. **[4 marks]**

The sample answer below would get 2 marks for giving two similar beliefs. Develop each point to gain 2 extra marks.

Christians might disagree with animal experimentation as humans are meant to be stewards over creation. ✓ **(1)**

_____

_____

_____

Muslims also disagree with animal experimentation because in a Hadith, Muhammad said you shouldn't kill anything bigger than a sparrow without just cause. ✓ **(1)**

_____

_____

_____

Theme C Explain **two** contrasting beliefs in contemporary British society about arguments from a scientific view against the existence of God.

In your answer you should refer to the main religious tradition of Great Britain and non-religious beliefs. **[4 marks]**

_____

_____

_____

_____

_____

_____

_____

_____

_____

TIP

The question says that you need to refer to the 'main religious tradition of Great Britain and non-religious beliefs'. So you could, for example, make one point about what Christians believe and then make a contrasting point about what atheists believe.

Theme D Explain **two** contrasting religious beliefs on pacifism.

In your answer you must refer to one or more religious traditions. **[4 marks]**

_____

_____

_____

_____

_____

_____

_____

_____

TIP

'In your answer you must refer to one or more religious traditions' means you need to mention at least one religion in your answer. For example, you could write about two contrasting beliefs within Christianity, or two contrasting beliefs within Islam. You can also mention more than one religion if you want, for example by contrasting a Christian belief with a Muslim belief.

Theme E Explain **two** contrasting beliefs in contemporary British society about the use of corporal punishment.

In your answer you should refer to the main religious tradition of Great Britain and one or more other religious traditions. **[4 marks]**

_____

_____

_____

_____

_____

_____

_____

_____

_____

TIP

Remember to make sure:
- your beliefs are contrasting (for example, one supports corporal punishment and one opposes it)
- you refer to Christianity ('the main religious tradition of Great Britain')
- you also mention another religion, such as Islam.

Theme F Explain two **similar** religious beliefs about giving money to the poor.

In your answer you must refer to one or more religious traditions. **[4 marks]**

_____

_____

_____

_____

_____

_____

_____

_____

TIP

Remember that developing a point does not mean making a new point – it means **adding detail** to the point you've already made. You could do this by giving an example, using a belief or teaching to back up the point, explaining why the point is important, or supporting it with a source of wisdom and authority.

Test the 5-mark question

Example

1 Explain **two** religious beliefs about freedom of religious expression.

Refer to sacred writings or another source of religious belief and teaching in your answer. **[5 marks]**

Christians believe we should be tolerant of all other beliefs. ✓ **(1)** *This is shown in the Bible in Romans 12:18 where it says 'if it is possible ... live at peace with everyone'.* ✓ **(1)** *This means that Christians should live in peace with those who express a different religious view to them.* ✓ **(1)**

Muslims believe that the whole of their life should be an expression of their religion. ✓ **(1)** *There are some divisions in Islam about how religious practices should be carried out, for example between Sunni and Shi'a Muslims, but most would say that this freedom shouldn't be restricted.* ✓ **(1)**

WHAT WILL THE QUESTION LOOK LIKE?

The 5-mark question will always start with the words **'Explain two…'** and end with the words **'Refer to sacred writings or another source of religious belief and teaching in your answer.'** A maximum of **5 marks** will be awarded.

HOW IS IT MARKED?

This answer would gain 5 marks because it makes two different points, and both points are developed. It also refers to a relevant source of religious belief and teaching.

(!) REMEMBER...

The 5-mark question is similar to the 4-mark question, so try to make **two different points** and **develop** each of them.

The additional instruction in the question asks you to **'refer to sacred writings or another source of religious belief and teaching in your answer'**. Try to think of a reference to a holy text (such as the Bible or Qur'an), the words of a prayer, or a quote from a religious leader that can back up one of your points. You only need one reference but can add more than one if you want.

Activity

Theme A Explain **two** religious beliefs about the purpose of families.

Refer to sacred writings or another source of religious belief and teaching in your answer. **[5 marks]**

The sample answer below would get 2 marks as there is one developed point. Complete the answer by adding a second developed point. For your fifth mark, add a reference to a source of religious belief and teaching. This could apply to either your first or second point.

For Christians, one purpose of the family is procreation. ✓ **(1)** *Having children fulfils God's plan for marriage.* ✓ **(1)**

_____

_____

_____

_____

_____

_____

_____

TIP

Remember that your source of religious belief and teaching needs to be relevant to the point you are making. For example, here you could refer to a passage in the Bible that suggests God wants married couples to have children.

| Theme B | Explain **two** religious beliefs about the origins of human life. |

Refer to sacred writings or another source of religious belief and teaching in your answer. **[5 marks]**

The sample answer below would get 5 marks because there are two points, each of which have been developed, and a reference to a source of religious belief and teaching. Add a tick next to each point. Then underline where each point has extra detail. Finally, draw a circle around a reference to a source of religious belief and teaching.

Some Christians believe that human life originated from Adam and Eve as it is described in the Bible, in the book of Genesis. It says that humans were made 'in God's image' which means that we have a special relationship with God.

Other Christians believe that the scientific theory of evolution tells us that humans have evolved over millions of years. They believe that science explains how humans got here but the Bible explains that God was responsible for this.

| Theme C | Explain **two** religious beliefs about evil and suffering. |

Refer to sacred writings or another source of religious belief and teaching in your answer. **[5 marks]**

TIP

You don't need to quote a source of religious belief and teaching word-for-word, but try to say where it came from. For example, whether it came from the Bible, a document produced by the Church, a speech by an Imam, etc.

Theme D Explain **two** religious beliefs about holy war.

Refer to sacred writings or another source of religious belief and teaching in your answer. **[5 marks]**

Theme E Explain **two** religious beliefs about retribution as an aim of punishment.

Refer to sacred writings or another source of religious belief and teaching in your answer. **[5 marks]**

Theme F | Explain **two** religious beliefs about racial prejudice and discrimination.

Refer to sacred writings or another source of religious belief and teaching in your answer.

[5 marks]

Test the 12-mark question

Example

1 'It is acceptable to use animals for experiments.'

Evaluate this statement.

In your answer you:

- should give reasoned arguments in support of this statement
- should give reasoned arguments to support a different point of view
- should refer to religious arguments
- may refer to non-religious arguments
- should reach a justified conclusion. **[12 marks]**
[SPaG 3 marks]

WHAT WILL THE QUESTION LOOK LIKE?

The 12-mark question will always ask you to **evaluate** a statement. The bullet points underneath the statement will tell you the things the examiner expects to see in your answer. Here, you need to give reasoned arguments for and against the statement, and should also refer to religious arguments. The final bullet will always ask you to 'reach a justified conclusion'.

HOW IS IT MARKED?

The examiner will mark your answer using a mark scheme based on level descriptors (see below).

In addition, 3 extra marks will be awarded for your **spelling, punctuation and grammar**, and your use of **specialist terminology** (SPaG). In your themes exam, the best of your 4 SPaG marks will be added to your total, so it's worth taking care to use your best written English.

 REMEMBER...

Evaluating means to make a judgement, using **evidence** to decide how convincing you find the statement to be.

You should consider **arguments in support of the statement**, and decide how convincing you think those are, giving at least one reason. You then need to consider **why some people might support a different point of view**, and decide how convincing they are, again giving at least one reason.

You might want to decide how convincing an argument is by considering where it comes from. Is it based on a source of Christian belief and teaching, such as a teaching from the Bible, or something advised by a religious leader? If so, you may decide this evidence strengthens the argument and therefore whether you would support or oppose the statement in the question.

You might decide an argument is weak because it is only a personal opinion, or a popular idea with no strong evidence to support it. This would make it difficult for you to use to support or oppose the statement in the question when reaching a judgement and you must explain the reasons why you reach your judgements.

To reach a **justified conclusion** you should consider both sides of the argument, and make your own judgement about which you find more convincing. You might conclude that each side has its own strengths. To make sure your conclusion is 'justified', you need to **give reasons or evidence to support your view**, but don't *just* repeat all the reasons and evidence you have already used.

Level descriptors

Level 1 (1–3 marks)	• Point of view with reason(s) stated in support.
Level 2 (4–6 marks)	• Reasoned consideration of a point of view. • A logical chain of reasoning drawing on knowledge and understanding of relevant evidence and information. OR • Recognition of different points of view, each supported by relevant reasons/evidence. • **Maximum of Level 2 if there is no reference to religion.**
Level 3 (7–9 marks)	• Reasoned consideration of different points of view. • Logical chains of reasoning that draw on knowledge and understanding of relevant evidence and information. • **Clear reference to religion.**
Level 4 (10–12 marks)	• A well-argued response, reasoned consideration of different points of view. • Logical chains of reasoning leading to judgement(s) supported by knowledge and understanding of relevant evidence and information. • **Reference to religion applied to the issue.**

2 When you answer a 12-mark question, the first thing to do is to read the statement carefully and think about what it is asking. You can quickly note down any ideas that you have on the topic. Here is an example of some notes a student has made in response to the statement 'It is acceptable to use animals for experiments.'

Different types of experiment? For make-up, for medicines to save lives, to advance science.

Some Christians – for the statement

- *Dominion. Genesis 1 – God told humans they have power over creation.*
- *Medical experiments help humans – 'love your neighbour', situation ethics.*
- *Humans are sacred – sanctity of life – animals should be used to help them.*

Some Muslims – against the statement

- *Qur'an – use animals for food and travel, doesn't mention experiments.*
- *Hadith – don't kill anything bigger than a sparrow without 'just cause'.*
- *Khalifah – Muslims are stewards.*
- *Muhammad treated animals well.*

Conclusion: depends on what experiments, matters how you treat them.

TIP

If you write down ideas to help you plan, make sure you cross them out so the examiner doesn't think they are your answer.

3 'Religious believers should do everything they can to make peace in the world.'

Evaluate this statement.

In your answer you:

- should give reasoned arguments in support of this statement
- should give reasoned arguments to support a different point of view
- should refer to religious arguments
- may refer to non-religious arguments
- should reach a justified conclusion.

[12 marks]
[SPaG 3 marks]

Use the space below to note down some ideas that you could use to answer the question above.

_____

_____

_____

_____

_____

_____

_____

_____

_____

4 Once you have planned your answer, you need to start writing it. In the example below, the student has taken their notes on the statement 'It is acceptable to use animals for experiments' and used it to write two sections – one that supports the statement and one that opposes it.

Some Christians would agree that it is acceptable to use animals for experiments as humans have dominion over creation, as it says in Genesis that God told Adam and Eve they have power over his creation.

This passage in the Bible strengthens the argument as it shows that God gave humans power over animals. Christians also believe that humans are sacred as they are made in God's image and animals aren't, so this supports the idea of dominion and using animals how we choose. Christians may also say that experimenting on animals for medical science would be supported by key Bible teachings such as 'love your neighbour', as you are trying to help people who are ill by finding a cure for their illness.

Many teachings in Christianity are about helping each other and as animal experimentation can be used to help people, we should use it to our advantage.

On the other hand, some Muslims would disagree with using animals for experiments as the Qur'an mentions using animals for food and for travel but it doesn't mention using them for experiments. The Qur'an is a reliable source for Muslims, although it is true that it doesn't mention many modern ethical issues. Muslims might also disagree with using animals for experiments as they are meant to be good stewards, which includes looking after animals. Muhammad was known to have treated animals well and he said in a Hadith that you shouldn't kill anything bigger than a sparrow without just cause. However, it could be argued that experimenting on animals to develop medicines is a just cause, so perhaps it depends on what the experimentation is for.

TIP Here the student has referred to a source of wisdom and authority to support their point. This shows the examiner that you are using relevant information and evidence.

TIP The student has applied religious views to the issue of animal experiments. You can only achieve a maximum of 6 marks if you don't refer to religious views.

TIP This paragraph shows how your answer can show logical chains of reasoning by giving different views. Think of it like a discussion, where someone gives their point and another person counters it with a different point.

5 Let's revisit the notes you wrote in response to the statement 'Religious believers should do everything they can to make peace in the world.' Now use your notes to write out one paragraph of arguments that could be used to support the statement, and one paragraph of arguments that could be used to oppose the statement.

6 Once you have evaluated the arguments for and against the statement, you need to write a conclusion where you give an overall judgement. This is where you decide whether overall you think the arguments for the statement are stronger or weaker than the arguments against it.

Consider these questions:

- Are the arguments for the different views strong or weak? Why?

- Is one view stronger than the other, or are they equal? Why?

- Is there a simple answer, or is it complicated? Why?

- What is your view on these arguments?

Here is an example of a conclusion in response to the statement, 'It is acceptable to use animals for experiments.'

In conclusion, I think that the arguments for using animals for experiments are stronger as they focus on dominion and how we can be loving to other humans, which is a key teaching in Christianity. However, I think that most religious people would only agree with these experiments if they are to help serious illnesses, not for unnecessary things like testing make-up. The arguments against animal experiments don't directly address using animals for experiments, they are more about treating animals kindly overall, and it is possible to treat animals well during the experimentation process. Overall many religious teachings lead us to believe it is acceptable to use animals for experiments that help to cure illnesses.

TIP

In their final paragraph the student has come to a justified conclusion. They have summarised the key ideas and views and come to a final judgement on the statement.

7 Now write your own conclusion in response to the statement, 'Religious believers should do everything they can to make peace in the world'.

TIP

In the conclusion you need to give your view on the statement, based on the views and arguments you have discussed.

8 This is what an answer might look like. Use the key below to see where the answer addresses the requirements of the mark scheme.

reasoned arguments in support of this statement
reasoned arguments to support a different point of view
supported by knowledge and understanding of relevant evidence and information – reference to sources of wisdom and authority
evaluation of arguments
a justified conclusion

'It is acceptable to use animals for experiments.'

Evaluate this statement.

In your answer you:

- should give reasoned arguments in support of this statement
- should give reasoned arguments to support a different point of view
- should refer to religious arguments
- may refer to non-religious arguments
- should reach a justified conclusion.

TIP
This example hasn't used non-religious arguments, but you are allowed to include these in a 12-mark question.

[12 marks]
[SPaG 3 marks]

Some Christians would agree that it is acceptable to use animals for experiments as humans have dominion over creation as in Genesis it says that God told Adam and Eve that they had power over his creation. This strengthens the argument as it shows that God gave humans this power. Christians also believe that humans were made in God's image and animals aren't, so this supports the idea of dominion and us using animals how we choose. They also may say that using animals to experiment on for medical science would be supported by key Bible teachings such as 'love your neighbour' as you are trying to help those people that are ill, by finding a medicine or a cure to their illness. This is supported by Situation Ethics as it would be doing the most loving thing for those that are sick. These strengthen the argument as many teachings in Christianity are about helping each other and as God gave us this knowledge, we should use it to our advantage.

On the other hand, some Muslims would disagree with using animals for experiments as the Qur'an mentions using animals for food and for travel not for experiments. The Qur'an is a reliable source for Muslims however just because it doesn't mention experiments it doesn't mean they are wrong. The Qur'an doesn't mention many modern ethical issues. They might also disagree with using animals for experiments as Muhammad was known to have treated animals well and he said in a Hadith, 'if you kill anything bigger than a sparrow you will be asked about it on Judgement Day'. However, this doesn't give strong support to the argument as it doesn't specifically say you cannot use animals, it just means that we should think carefully about it as Allah will ask us about it at judgement.

In conclusion, I think that the arguments for using animals for experiments are stronger as they focus on dominion and how we can be loving to other humans which is a key teaching in Christianity. However, I think that most religious people would only agree with these experiments if they are to help serious illnesses not for unnecessary things like testing make-up. The arguments against animal experiments don't directly address using animals for experiments and it is possible to treat them well during the process. Allah may well have given us this knowledge to allow us to help one another, which the Qur'an also supports. Overall many religious teachings lead us to believe it is acceptable to use animals for experiments that help to cure illnesses.

TIP
Look at how this 12 mark answer is presented. It has three clear paragraphs: one in support of the statement, one supporting a different point of view and finally a justified conclusion. This is the easiest way to write your answer.

TIP
You can evaluate arguments throughout your answer. It doesn't have to be left until the conclusion.

TIP
The conclusion can summarise which arguments are stronger or weaker and why. Alternatively, it might say how they are equally strong/weak and why. This shows an overall judgment on the statement.

9 Now look over the paragraphs you wrote on pages 142–144. Have you addressed the requirements of the mark scheme?

Use the key above and use colours to highlight your own paragraph to check where you address the requirements of the mark scheme.

10 For the themes you are studying, answer these 12-mark questions.

Theme A: Relationships and families	'Men and women should be treated differently'
Theme B: Religion and life	'Religious believers are the only people that have a duty to protect the world'
Theme C: The existence of God and revelation	'We can see God in nature'
Theme D: Religion, peace and conflict	'Justice is more important than peace'
Theme E: Religion, crime and punishment	'Using the principle of utility is the best way to decide who should have the death penalty'
Theme F: Religion, human rights and social justice	'A religious person should only practise their religion in private'

Evaluate this statement.

In your answer you:

- should give reasoned arguments in support of this statement
- should give reasoned arguments to support a different point of view
- should refer to religious arguments
- may refer to non-religious arguments
- should reach a justified conclusion.

TIP

Remember, you will need to answer on 4 themes for your exam. Use these practice questions for the themes you have studied.

OXFORD
UNIVERSITY PRESS

Great Clarendon Street, Oxford, OX2 6DP, United Kingdom

Oxford University Press is a department of the University of Oxford.
It furthers the University's objective of excellence in research,
scholarship, and education by publishing worldwide. Oxford is a
registered trade mark of Oxford University Press in the UK and in
certain other countries

© Oxford University Press 2019

The moral rights of the authors have been asserted

First published in 2019

British Library Cataloguing in Publication Data

Data available

978-0-19-844566-1

10 9 8 7 6 5 4 3 2

Paper used in the production of this book is a natural, recyclable
product made from wood grown in sustainable forests.

The manufacturing process conforms to the environmental regula-
tions of the country of origin.

Printed in China by Golden Cup

Acknowledgements
We are grateful to the authors and publishers for use of extracts
from their titles and in particular for the following:

Scripture quotations [marked NIV] taken from the **Holy Bible, New
International Version Anglicised** Copyright © 1979, 1984, 2011
Biblica. Used by permission of Hodder & Stoughton Ltd, an Hachette
UK company. All rights reserved; Excerpts from **Catechism of the
Catholic Church**, http://www.vatican.va/archive/ccc_css/archive/
catechism/ccc_toc.htm (Strathfield, NSW: St Pauls, 2000). © Libreria
Editrice Vaticana. Reproduced with permission from The Vatican;
Excerpts from **The Qur'an OWC** translated by M. A. S. Abdel
Haleem (Oxford University Press, 2008). © M. A. S. Abdel Haleem
2004, 2005. Reproduced with permission from Oxford University
Press; **The Church of England:** *The Lambeth Conference: Resolutions
Archive from 1930*, (Anglican Communion Office, 2005). Reproduced
with permission from The Lambeth Conference; **Church of En-
gland:** Official Church of England submission in response to the
Government's intention to introduce same-sex marriage, June 2012
(Church of England, 2012). Copyright © The Archbishops' Council.
Reproduced with permission from The Archbishops' Council; **Pope
Paul VI:** *Humanae Vitae, On the Regulation of Birth*, July 25th 1968
(The Vatican, 1968). © Libreria Editrice Vaticana. Reproduced with
permission from The Vatican; **Quakers in Britain:** *Quaker Faith
and Practice*, fifth edition, (Quakers in Britain,1989). Reproduced
with permission from the Yearly Meeting of the Religious Society of
Friends (Quakers) in Britain.

Cover: Image Source/Getty; Maskot/Offset

Illustrations: Jason Ramasami, QBS Learning

Photos: p84: MikeDotta/Shutterstock; **p104:** Alamy/epa european
pressphoto agency b.v; **p112:** Darrin Henry/Shutterstock

We have made every effort to trace and contact all copyright holders
before publication, but if notified of any errors or omissions, the
publisher will be happy to rectify these at the earliest opportunity.

Links to third party websites are provided by Oxford in good faith
and for information only. Oxford disclaims any responsibility for the
materials contained in any third party website referenced in this work.

Please note that the practice questions in this book allow students a
genuine attempt at practising exam skills, but they are not intended
to replicate examination papers.

Thank you
OUP wishes to thank Aisha Mohammad and Julie Haigh for their
help reviewing this book.